English Grammar for Students of French

The Study Guide
for Those Learning French

Fourth edition

Jacqueline Morton

A member of the Hodder Headline Group
LONDON • AUCKLAND

English Grammar for Students of Languages Series
Edited by Jacqueline Morton

First published in the United States of America by
The Olivia and Hill Press

First published in Great Britain in 1999 by
Arnold, a member of the Hodder Headline Group,
338 Euston Road, London NW1 3BH

http://www.arnoldpublishers.com

©1997 Jacqueline Morton

British Library Cataloguing in Publication Data
A catalogue record for this book is available from the British Library

ISBN 0 340 74202 X

1 2 3 4 5 6 7 8 9 10

Printed and bound in the United States of America

What do you think about this book? Or any other Arnold title?
Please send your comments to feedback.arnold@hodder.co.uk

CONTENTS

CONTENTS

CONTENTS

To the Student

English Grammar for Students of French explains the grammatical terms that are in your French textbook and shows you how they relate to English grammar. Once you have understood the terms and concepts in your own language, it will be easier for you to undertand what is being introduced in French. This handbook also points out the similarities and differences between English and French grammar and alerts you to common pitfalls.

Most teachers incorporate *English Grammar* into the class syllabus so that you will know which pages to read before doing a French assignment. If you are selecting the pages yourself, check the detailed index for the terms and concepts you will need for your assignment. When you finish a chapter in this handbook, you can test your comprehension by doing the short *Reviews* and checking your answers against the *Answer Key* (see p. 165).

TIPS FOR STUDYING A FOREIGN LANGUAGE

1. **RULES** — Make sure you understand each rule before moving on to the next one. Language learning is like building a house; each brick is only as secure as its foundation.

2. **MEMORIZATION** — Students often think that if they read French words and conjugations over and over again they "know" them. Reading will only enable you to recognize them, if you see them. It is only by memorizing that you will be able to produce them. Here are the steps you should follow:

    1. Divide the words or conjugation to be memorized into small groups, 3 or 4 words at a time for instance.
    2. Read the first group of words aloud several times.
    3. Write them down as you repeat them aloud to yourself.
    4. Compare what you wrote with the original.
    5. Repeat steps 2-4 until there is no difference between what you said or wrote and the original.
    6. Continue memorizing each group of words in the same way, reciting from the beginning each time.

Never memorize something you don't understand.

3. **VOCABULARY** — Use any trick or gimmick that will help you remember new words. Here are some that students have found useful:

- Write each word on a separate index card, French on one side, English on the other.
- Use index cards or pens of different colors. To help you remember gender, use blue for masculine nouns and red for feminine nouns. If you wish to remember parts of speech, you can use green for verbs, orange for adjectives, etc.
- Group the cards by meaning or characteristics. For example, food vocabulary can be divided into fruits, meats, desserts, foods you like, foods you don't like, etc. Whatever categories you wish.
- To review, look at the English word. Say the corresponding French word aloud (or write it), and flip the card to check your answer. Shuffle the deck often so that the English words come up in different order.

4. **WRITTEN EXERCISES** — Read the French words and sentences out loud as you write them. That way you are practicing seeing, saying, and hearing the words. It will help you remember them.

5. **DAILY PRACTICE** — Don't get behind. It's almost impossible to catch up in language learning because you need daily practice and time to absorb the material.

6. **LANGUAGE TAPES** — It is better to listen to tapes for short periods several times during the week rather than doing everything in one long session.

Bonne chance,

Jacqueline Morton

P.S. Keep in touch. Send me your comments, suggestions, and questions via e-mail: jmorton@umich.edu.

INTRODUCTION

When you learn a foreign language, in this case French, you must look at each word in three ways: MEANING, PART OF SPEECH, and FUNCTION.

MEANING

An English word may be connected to a French word that has a similar meaning.

> *Boy*, a young male child, has the same meaning as the French word **garçon**.

Words with equivalent meanings are learned by memorizing vocabulary. Sometimes two words are the same or very similar in both English and French. These words are called **COGNATES** and are, of course, easy to learn.

ENGLISH	FRENCH
intelligent	intelligent
government	gouvernement
continue	continuer

Occasionally knowing one French word will help you learn another.

> Knowing that **chanter** is *to sing* should help you learn that **un chanteur** is *a singer*.

Usually there is little similarity between words, and knowing one French word will not help you learn another. As a general rule, you must memorize each vocabulary item separately.

> Knowing that **homme** is *man* will not help you learn that **femme** is *woman*.

In addition, every language has its own expressions; these are called **IDIOMATIC EXPRESSIONS**, or **IDIOMS**. For instance, "*to fall* asleep" and "*to take* a walk" are English expressions where "*to fall*" and "*to take*" do not have their usual meaning as in "*to fall* down the stairs," or "*to take* a book to school." You will have to be on the alert for these idioms because they cannot be translated word-for-word in French.

The French equivalent of the English idiom "to fall asleep" is "s'endormir" [literally, *to put oneself to sleep*] and "to take a walk" is equivalent to the French idiom "**faire une promenade**" [literally "*to make* a walk"].

PART OF SPEECH

In English and French a word can be classified as belonging to one of eight categories called PARTS OF SPEECH:

noun	article
verb	adverb
pronoun	preposition
adjective	conjunction

Some parts of speech are further broken down according to type. Adjectives, for instance, can be descriptive, interrogative, demonstrative, or possessive. Each part of speech has its own rules for spelling, pronunciation, and use.

In order to choose the correct French equivalent of an English word, you will have to identify its part of speech. For example, look at the word *what* and its French equivalents in the following sentences:

What do you want?
|
interrogative pronoun → **qu'est-ce que**

What movie did you see?
|
interrogative adjective → **quel**

I'll do *what* you want.
|
relative pronoun → **ce que**

The English word is the same in all three sentences. In French, however, three different words are used and three different sets of rules apply because each *what* belongs to a different part of speech.

FUNCTION

In English and French the role a word plays in a sentence is called its FUNCTION. Depending on the sentence, the same word can have a variety of functions:

subject
direct object
indirect object
object of a preposition

Let us go back again to the word *what* and see the various functions it can have in a sentence.

> *What* is on the table?
>
> sub|ject → **qu'est-ce qui**

80

> *What* is she doing?
>
> dire|ct object → **qu'est-ce que**

> *What* are you talking about?
>
> obj|ect of preposition → **de quoi**

The English word is the same in all three sentences. In French, however, three different words are used because each *what* has a different function.

90

In order to choose the correct French equivalent of an English word, you will have to identify its function.

SUMMARY

As a student of French you must learn to recognize both the part of speech and the function of each word in a given sentence. This is essential because words in a French sentence have a great deal of influence on one another.

> *The beautiful white* **car** *belongs to my big brother.*

> La belle **voiture** blanche appartient à mon grand **frère**.

100

In English, the only word that affects another word in the sentence is *car*, which forces us to say *belongs*. If the word were *cars*, we would have to say *belong*.

In French, the word for *car* (**voiture**) not only affects the word for *belongs* (**appartient**), but also the spelling and pronunciation of the French words for *the* (**la**), *beautiful* (**belle**), and *white* (**blanche**). The word for *brother* (**frère**) affects the spelling and pronunciation of the French words for *my* (**mon**), and *big* (**grand**).

110

Since parts of speech and function are determined in the same way in English and in French, this handbook will show you how to identify them in English. Then, you will learn to analyze English and French constructions, focussing on similarities and differences. This will give you a better understanding of the explanations in your French textbook.

CHAPTER

1

WHAT IS A NOUN?

A **NOUN** is a word that can be the name of a person, animal, place, thing, event or idea.

- a person
  professor, clown, student, girl
  Professor Smith, Bozo, Paul, Mary
- an animal
  dog, bird, bear, snake
  Heidi, Tweetie, Teddy
- a place
  city, state, country, continent
  stadium, restaurant, France, Europe
- a thing
  lamp, airplane, book, dress
  Perrier, Eiffel Tower, Arch of Triumph
- an event or activity
  graduation, marriage, birth, death
  football, robbery, rest, growth
- an idea or concept
  poverty, democracy, humor, mathematics
  addition, strength, elegance, virtue

As you can see, a noun is not only a word which names something that is tangible (i.e., that you can touch), such as *table, dog,* and *White House,* it can also be the name of things that are abstract (i.e., that you cannot touch), such as *justice, jealousy,* and *honor.*

A noun that does not state the name of a specific person, place, thing, etc. is called a **COMMON NOUN.** A common noun does not begin with a capital letter, unless it is the first word of a sentence. All the words above that are not capitalized are common nouns.

A noun that is the name of a specific person, place, thing, etc. is called a **PROPER NOUN.** A proper noun always begins with a capital letter. All the words above that are capitalized are proper nouns.

Mary is a girl.
proper   common
noun   noun

A noun that is made up of two words is called a **COMPOUND NOUN.** A compound noun can be composed of two common nouns, such as *comic strip* and *ice cream* or two proper nouns, such as *North America.*

IN ENGLISH ────────────────────────────────

To help you learn to recognize nouns, look at the paragraph below where the nouns are in *italics*.

> The best *purchases* from *France* include *wines, perfumes,*
> *scarves, gloves* and other luxury *items*. Today, French
> *workers* make excellent *skis* and *tennis rackets* which are
> sold the *world* over. Thanks to the *Common Market*,
> you can find *goods* from *Germany, Italy, England,* and
> their commercial *partners* in all large French *stores*.
> Thus, Italian *sportscars*, English *leather*, German *glass-*
> *ware*, and Belgian *lace* can be bought at *prices* compa-
> rable to those in the *country* of *origin*.

40

IN FRENCH ────────────────────────────────

Nouns are identified in the same way as they are in
English.

50

──────────── **TERMS USED TO TALK ABOUT NOUNS** ────────────

- **GENDER** — A noun has a gender; that is, it can be classified according to whether it is masculine, feminine, or neuter (see *What is Meant by Gender?*, p. 6).

- **NUMBER** — A noun has a number; that is, it can be identified according to whether it is singular or plural (see *What is Meant by Number?*, p. 9).

- **COUNT OR NON-COUNT** — A noun can be classified as to whether it is a count noun or non-count noun; that is, whether it refers to something that can be counted or not (see p. 14 in *What are Articles?*).

60

- **FUNCTION** — A noun can have a variety of functions in a sentence; that is, it can be the subject of the sentence (see *What is a Subject?*, p. 24) or an object (see *What are Objects?*, p. 104).

── *R E V I E W* ──

Circle the nouns in the following sentences:

1. The boy came into the classroom and spoke to the teacher.
2. The textbook has a painting on its cover.
3. Mary Evans visited Paris with her class.
4. The lion roared and the children screamed.
5. Truth is stranger than fiction.
6. His kindness and understanding were known throughout the world.

CHAPTER

2

WHAT IS MEANT BY GENDER?

1   GENDER in the grammatical sense means that a word can be classified as masculine, feminine, or neuter.

> Did Paul give Mary the book?
> Yes, *he* gave *it* to *her.*
> | | |
>   masc. neuter fem.

Gender is not very important in English; however, it is at the very heart of the French language where the gender of a word is often reflected not only in the way the word
10 itself is spelled and pronounced, but also in the way all the words connected to it are spelled and pronounced.

    More parts of speech have a gender in French than in English.

ENGLISH	FRENCH
pronouns	nouns
possessive adjectives	articles
	pronouns
	adjectives

    Since each part of speech follows its own rules to indi-
20 cate gender, you will find gender discussed in the chapters dealing with articles and the various types of pronouns and adjectives. In this section we shall only look at the gender of nouns.

IN ENGLISH————————————————————————

Nouns themselves do not have a gender, but sometimes their meaning indicates a gender based on the biological sex of the person or animal the noun stands for. For instance, when we replace a proper or common noun which refers to a man or a woman, we use *he* for males
30 and *she* for females.

- nouns referring to males indicate the MASCULINE gender

> Paul came home; *he* was tired, and I was glad to see *him.*
> | | |
> noun (male)   masculine   masculine

- nouns referring to females indicate the FEMININE gender

> Mary came home; *she* was tired, and I was glad to see *her.*
> | | |
> noun (female) feminine   feminine

All the proper or common nouns which do not have a biological gender are considered **NEUTER** and are replaced by *it*. ⁴⁰

> The city of Washington is lovely. I enjoyed visiting *it*.
> |
>   noun   neuter

IN FRENCH

All nouns — common nouns and proper nouns — have a gender; they are either masculine or feminine. Do not confuse the grammatical terms "masculine" and "feminine" with the terms "male" and "female." Only a few French nouns have a grammatical gender tied to whether ⁵⁰ they refer to someone of the male or female sex, most nouns have a gender which must be memorized.

The gender of common and proper nouns based on **BIOLOGICAL GENDER** is easy to determine. These are nouns whose meaning can only refer to one or the other of the biological sexes, male or female.

MALES → MASCULINE	FEMALES → FEMININE
Paul	Mary
boy	girl
brother	sister
son	daughter

The gender of all other nouns, common and proper, cannot be explained or figured out. These nouns only have a **GRAMMATICAL GENDER** which is unrelated to biological sex and which must be memorized. Here are some examples of English nouns classified under the gender of their French equivalent.

MASCULINE	FEMININE
boat	car
suicide	death
Japan	France
blackboard	chalk
government	democracy

As you learn a new noun, you should always learn its gender because it will affect the spelling and pronunciation of the words related to it. Textbooks and dictionaries usually indicate the gender of a noun with an *m.* for masculine or an *f.* for feminine. Sometimes the indefinite articles are used: *un* for masculine or *une* for feminine (see ⁸⁰ *What are Articles?*, p. 11).

CAREFUL — Do not rely on biological gender to indicate the grammatical gender of French equivalents of nouns which can refer to a man or a woman. For instance, the grammatical gender of the noun "**professeur**" *(professor)* is always masculine, even though the person being referred to could be a man or woman.

— REVIEW —

Circle M (masculine) or F (feminine) next to the nouns whose gender you can identify, and (?) next to the nouns whose gender you would have to look up in a dictionary.

GENDER IN FRENCH

	M	F	?
1. boys	(M)	F	?
2. chair	M	F	(?)
3. Jane	M	(F)	?
4. classroom	M	F	(?)
5. visitor	M	F	(?)
6. sisters	M	(F)	?
7. houses	M	F	(?)

WHAT IS MEANT BY NUMBER?

NUMBER in the grammatical sense means that a word can be
classified as singular or plural. When a word refers
to one person or thing, it is said to be **SINGULAR**;
when it refers to more than one, it is **PLURAL**.

one *book*	two *books*
singular	plural

More parts of speech indicate number in French than
in English and there are more spelling and pronunciation
changes in French than in English.

ENGLISH	FRENCH
nouns	nouns
verbs	verbs
pronouns	pronouns
demonstrative adjectives	adjectives
	articles

Since each part of speech follows its own rules to indicate number, you will find number discussed in the chapters dealing with articles, the various types of adjectives
and pronouns, as well as in all the sections on verbs. In
this section we shall only look at the number of nouns.

IN ENGLISH

A singular noun is made plural in one of two ways:

1. some singular nouns add an "*-s*" or "*-es*"

book	books
kiss	kisses

2. other singular nouns change their spelling

man	men
mouse	mice
leaf	leaves
child	children

Some nouns, called **COLLECTIVE NOUNS**, refer to a group of
persons or things, but the noun itself is considered singular.

A football *team* has eleven players.
The *family* is well.

IN FRENCH

As in English, the plural form of a noun is usually spelled differently from the singular.

The most common change is the same as the one made in English; that is, an "-s" is added to the singular masculine or feminine noun.

	SINGULAR	PLURAL		
MASCULINE	livre	livres	*book*	*books*
FEMININE	table	tables	*table*	*tables*

Some nouns indicate the plural differently. When that is the case, your textbook will give you the plural form.

HEARING THE PLURAL

In English you can always hear the plural in the noun itself.

SINGULAR	PLURAL
the **book**	the **books**
the **child**	the **children**

In French, even though you can always see the plural ending of the noun, you don't usually hear it in the noun itself because the final "s" is not pronounced.

same pronunciation

livre	livres
enfant	enfants

To know whether the noun is singular or plural, you will have to listen to the word that comes before the noun.

le livre	**les** livres
l'enfant	**les** enfants

— REVIEW —

Look at the English and French words below. Under Column A indicate if the word is singular (S) or plural (P).

- Say the English and French words aloud. Under Column B indicate if you can hear if the word is singular (S) or plural (P) or if you can't tell (?).

	Column A		Column B		
1. desks	S	(P)	S	(P)	?
2. maisons	S	(P)	S	P	(?)
3. tooth	(S)	P	(S)	P	?
4. feet	S	(P)	S	(P)	?
5. étudiantes	S	(P)	S	P	(?)

4

WHAT ARE ARTICLES?

An ARTICLE is a word placed before a noun to show whether
the noun refers to a specific person, animal, place, thing,
event or idea, or whether it refers to a nonspecific
person, thing, or idea. [1]

> I saw *the* boy you spoke about.
> |
> a specific boy

> I saw *a* boy in the street.
> |
> a nonspecific boy [10]

In English and French there are two types of articles,
DEFINITE ARTICLES and INDEFINITE ARTICLES.

─────────── **DEFINITE ARTICLES** ───────────

IN ENGLISH

A DEFINITE ARTICLE is used before a noun when we are speaking about a specific person, place, animal, thing, or idea.
There is one definite article, *the*.

> I read *the* book you recommended. [20]
> |
> a specific book

> I ate *the* apple you gave me.
> |
> a specific apple

The definite article remains *the* even when the noun
which follows becomes plural.

> I read *the books* you recommended.
> I ate *the apples* you gave me.

IN FRENCH [30]

As in English, a definite article is used before a noun when
referring to a specific person, place, animal, thing, or idea.
In French, it is also used when speaking in general terms.

> J'aime **les** chiens mais je déteste **les** chats.
> *I like dogs but I hate cats.*

> **Les** chiens sont plus fidèles que **les** chats.
> *Dogs are more faithful than cats.*

In French, the article works hand-in-hand with the noun to which it belongs in that it matches the noun's gender and number. This "matching" is called AGREEMENT. One says that "the article *agrees* with the noun." (see *What is Meant by Gender?*, p. 6 and *What is Meant by Number?*, p. 9).

A different article is used, therefore, depending on whether the noun is masculine or feminine (gender) and on whether the noun is singular or plural (number). Because these various forms of the articles are both pronounced and spelled differently, they indicate the gender and number of the noun to the ear as well as to the eye (see p. 10 regarding the "hearing" of the plural in French).

There are four forms of the definite article: three singular forms and one plural.

- **le** indicates that the noun is masculine singular

le livre	*the book*
le garçon	*the boy*

- **la** indicates that the noun is feminine singular

la table	*the table*
la pomme	*the apple*

- **l'** is used instead of **le** and **la** before a word beginning with a vowel.[1] It does not tell us, therefore, if the noun is masculine or feminine.

  l'étudiant   *the student*
  |
  masculine

  l'université   *the university*
  |
  feminine

The letter "h" is never pronounced. When a word starts with "h", it is usually considered as beginning with a vowel: **l'hiver** *(the winter)*; **l'hôtel** *(the hotel)*. Your textbook will go into the few exceptions to this rule.

- **les** is used to indicate that the noun is plural. Since there is only one form, it does not tell us if the noun is masculine or feminine.

les livres	*the books*
les tables	*the tables*

[1]Vowels are the sounds associated with the letters *a, e, i (y), o* and *u;* consonants are the sounds associated with the other letters of the alphabet.

INDEFINITE ARTICLES

IN ENGLISH

An **INDEFINITE ARTICLE** is used before a noun when we are not speaking about a specific person, animal, place, thing, event, or idea. There are two indefinite articles, *a* and *an*.

- *a* is used before a word beginning with a consonant

> I saw *a* boy in the street.
> |
> not a specific boy

- *an* is used before a word beginning with a vowel

> I ate *an* apple.
> |
> not a specific apple

The indefinite article is used only with a singular noun. To indicate a nonspecific plural noun, the word *some* can be used, but is usually not necessary.

> I saw boys in the street.
> I saw *(some)* boys in the street.

> I ate apples.
> I ate *(some)* apples.

IN FRENCH

As in English, an indefinite article is used before a noun when we are not speaking about a specific person, animal, place, thing, event, or idea.

Just as with definite articles, indefinite articles must agree with the noun's gender and number.

There are three forms of the indefinite article: two singular forms and one plural.

- **un** indicates that the noun is masculine singular

> **un** livre   *a book*
> **un** garçon   *a boy*

- **une** indicates that the noun is feminine singular

> **une** table   *a table*
> **une** pomme   *an apple*

- **des** is used to indicate that the noun is plural. Since there is only one form, it does not tell us if the noun is masculine or feminine.

> **des** livres   *(some) books*
> **des** tables   *(some) tables*

80

90

100

110

120

PARTITIVE ARTICLES

French also has another set of articles called **PARTITIVE ARTI-CLES** because they refer to *"part of the whole."* Partitive articles can be translated by the words *some* or *any,* but they are often left out in English.

Partitive articles are used before certain nouns called **NON-COUNT NOUNS.** As the name implies, a non-count noun designates an object that cannot be counted. For example, the noun *water* is a non-count noun because it is a noun which cannot be preceded by numbers such as 1, 2, 3, etc. (You cannot count *one water, two waters...*). Since a non-count noun cannot be counted, it is always singular.

Partitive articles are not used before **COUNT NOUNS,** nouns designating objects that can be counted. For example, the noun *pen* can be preceded by numbers such as 1, 2, 3, etc. (*one pen, two pens...*). Since a count noun can be counted, it can be singular or plural.

Like all articles in French, partitive articles agree with the noun's gender and number. Since non-count nouns don't have a plural form and are always singular, partitive articles only have singular forms.

There are three forms of the partitive article: masculine singular, feminine singular, and preceding a vowel.

- **du** indicates that the noun is masculine singular

> J'achète **du** beurre.
> *I am buying (some) butter.*
>
> Voulez-vous **du** beurre?
> *Do you want (any) butter?*

- **de la** indicates that the noun is feminine singular

> J'achète **de la** viande.
> *I am buying (some) meat.*
>
> Voulez-vous **de la** viande?
> *Do you want (any) meat?*

- **de l'** is used instead of **du** and **de la** before a word beginning with a vowel. It does not tell us if the noun is masculine or feminine.

> Je bois **de l'**eau.
> |
>   feminine
> *I am drinking (some) water.*

130

140

150

160

Devez-vous **de l'**argent à Marie?
|
masculine
Do you owe (any) money to Mary?

The above is a brief summary of partitive articles. Refer to your textbook for the rules regarding their usage.

CAREFUL — Unlike English where a noun can be used without an article (*Truth* is stranger than *fiction*; *France* is a beautiful country), French nouns are usually preceded by an article: definite, indefinite or partitive.

170

— *REVIEW* —

Below is a list of English nouns preceded by a definite or indefinite article.

- Circle which of the nouns below are count nouns (C) and which are non-count nouns (N).
- Write the French article for each noun on the line provided. The French DICTIONARY ENTRY shows you if the noun (n.) is masculine (m.) or feminine (f.).

			DICTIONARY ENTRY	FRENCH ARTICLE
1. the books	Ⓒ	N	livre (n.m.)	Les
2. the friend	Ⓒ	N	ami (n.m.)	L'
3. some chairs	Ⓒ	N	chaise (n.f.)	des
4. an idea	Ⓒ	N	idée (n.f.)	une
5. some money	C	Ⓝ	argent (n.m.)	de l'
6. the weather	C	Ⓝ	temps (n.m.)	le
7. a course	Ⓒ	N	cours (n.m.)	Un
8. some luck	C	Ⓝ	chance (n.f.)	de la
9. the dinner	Ⓒ	N	dîner (n.m.)	le

WHAT IS THE POSSESSIVE?

1

The term **POSSESSIVE** means that one noun
owns or *possesses* another noun.

Mary's French book is on the table.
possessor   possessed

The tree's branches are broken.
possessor   possessed

IN ENGLISH ——————————————————————————

10

There are two constructions to show possession.

1. An apostrophe can be used. In this construction, the
possessor comes before the possessed.

- singular possessor adds an apostrophe + "s"

    Mary's dress
    a tree's branches

    singular possessor

- plural possessor ending with "s" adds an apostrophe
after the "s"

20

    the students' teacher
    the girls' club

    plural possessor

- a plural possessor not ending with "s" adds an apostrophe + "s"

    the children's playground
    the men's department

    plural possessor

30

2. The word *of* can be used. In this structure, the possessed comes before the possessor.

- a singular or plural possessor is preceded by *of the* or
of a

    the book *of the* professor
    the branches *of a* tree

    singular possessor

the teacher *of the* students
|
plural possessor

IN FRENCH————————————————————————————

There is only one way to express possession and that is by using the "of" construction (2 above). The apostrophe structure (1 above) does not exist.

The French structure parallels the English structure: the noun possessed + **de** ("of") + definite or indefinite article + the noun possessor.

Mary's dress
   | |
 possessor possessed
	la robe **de** Marie
	    | |
	 possessed possessor
	 the dress of Mary

the professor's book	le livre **du** professeur
	        |
	      de + le
	 the book of the professor

the woman's purse	le sac **de la** dame *the purse of the lady*
a tree's branches	les branches **d'un** arbre *the branches of a tree*

the students' teacher	le professeur **des** étudiants
	          |
	        de + les
	 the professor of the students

CAREFUL — Do not confuse **du, de la, de l'**, and **des** meaning *of* and *of the* with words of the same spelling which are partitive articles (see p. 14) and the plural indefinite article (p. 13) meaning *some* or *any*. When they indicate possession, they usually come between two nouns, *(the book* of the *teacher* → **le livre** du **professeur**).

— REVIEW —

Below are possessives using the apostrophe. Write the alternate English structure which is the word-for-word equivalent of the French structure.

1. some children's parents

The parents of some children

2. the dress's color

The colour of the dress'

3. the school's entrance

The entrance of the school

4. a car's speed

The speed of the car

5. the books' covers

The covers of the books

WHAT IS A VERB?

A **VERB** is a word that indicates the action of the sentence.   ₁
The word "action" is used in its broadest sense,
not necessarily physical action.

Let us look at different types of words which are verbs:

- a physical activity   to run, to hit, to talk, to walk
- a mental activity   to hope, to believe, to imagine, to dream, to think
- a condition   to be, to feel, to have, to seem

Many verbs, however, do not fall neatly into one of the   ₁₀
above three categories. They are verbs nevertheless
because they represent the "action" of the sentence.

> The book *costs* only $5.00.
> |
> to cost

> The students *seem* tired.
> |
> to seem

The verb is the most important word in a sentence. You
cannot write a **COMPLETE SENTENCE**, that is, express a com-   ₂₀
plete thought, without a verb.

It is important to identify verbs because the function of
words in a sentence often depends on the word's relationship to the verb. For instance, the subject of a sentence is
the word doing the action of the verb, and the object is
the word receiving the action of the verb (see *What is a
Subject?*, p. 24, and *What are Objects?*, p. 104) .

IN ENGLISH ————————————————————

To help you learn to recognize verbs, look at the paragraph below where verbs are in *italics*.   ₃₀

> The three students *entered* the restaurant, *selected* a
> table, *hung* up their coats and *sat* down. They
> *looked* at the menu and *asked* the waitress what she
> *recommended*. She *advised* the daily special, beef
> stew. It *was* not expensive. They *chose* a bottle of
> red wine and *ordered* a salad. The service *was* slow,
> but the food *tasted* very good. Good cooking, they

decided, takes time. They *ate* pastry for dessert and
finished the meal with coffee. They *felt* happy!

IN FRENCH

Verbs are identified the same way as they are in English.

────────── **TERMS USED TO TALK ABOUT VERBS** ──────────

- **INFINITIVE** OR **DICTIONARY FORM** — The verb form which is
  the name of the verb is called an infinitive: *to eat, to
  sleep, to drink* (see *What is an Infinitive?*, p. 21). In the dictionary a verb is listed without the "to": *eat, sleep, drink*.

- **CONJUGATION** — A verb is conjugated or changes in form
  to agree with its subject: *I do, he does* (see *What is a Verb
  Conjugation?*, p. 33).

- **TENSE** — A verb indicates tense; that is, the time (present, past, or future) of the action: *I am, I was, I will be*
  (see *What is Meant by Tense?*, p. 49).

- **MOOD** — A verb shows mood; that is, the speaker's attitude toward what he or she is saying (see *What is Meant
  by Mood?*, p. 69).

- **VOICE** — A verb shows voice; that is, the relation
  between the subject and the action of the verb (see
  What is Meant by Active and Passive Voice?, p. 160).

- **PARTICIPLE** — A verb may be used to form a participle:
  writing, written; singing, sung (see *What is a Participle?*,
  p. 53).

- **TRANSITIVE** OR **INTRANSITIVE** — A verb can be classified as
  transitive or intransitive depending on whether or not
  the verb can take a direct object (see *What are Objects?*,
  p. 104).

— *REVIEW* —

Circle the verbs in the following sentences.

1. The students purchase their lunch at school.

2. Paul and Mary were happy.

3. They enjoyed the movie, but they preferred the book.

4. Paul ate dinner, finished his novel, and then went to bed.

5. It was sad to see the little dog struggle to get out of the lake.

6. I attended a concert to celebrate the New Year.

WHAT IS THE INFINITIVE?

The INFINITIVE form is the name of the verb.

The French equivalent of the verb *to learn* is **étudier**.
                                                ⌐⎯⌐
                                             infinitive

IN ENGLISH

The infinitive is composed of two words: *to* + the dictionary form of the verb *(to speak, to dance)*. By DICTIONARY FORM we mean the form of the verb that is listed as the entry in the dictionary *(speak, dance)*.

Although the infinitive is the most basic form of the verb, it can never be used in a sentence without another verb which is conjugated (see *What is a Verb Conjugation?*, p. 33).

To learn is exciting.
⌐⎯⌐ ⌐
infinitive conjugated verb

It *is* important *to be* on time.
⌐ ⌐⎯⌐
conjugated verb infinitive

Paul and Mary *want to dance* together.
⌐ ⌐⎯⌐
conjugated verb infinitive

The dictionary form of the verb, rather than the infinitive, is used after a verb such as *must, let* and *can.*

Paul *must be* home by noon.
⌐
dictionary form

Mr. Smith *lets* his daughter *watch* television.
⌐
dictionary form

IN FRENCH

The infinitive form is usually shown by the last two or three letters of the verb called THE ENDING.

dan**ser**	*to dance*
fin**ir**	*to finish*
ven**dre**	*to sell*
rece**voir**	*to receive*

1

10

20

30

The infinitive form is important not only because it is the form under which a verb is listed in the dictionary, but because the ending, called LA TERMINAISON, indicates the pattern the verb will follow to create its various forms.

1ˢᵗ CONJUGATION — verbs ending in -er follow one pattern
2ᴺᴰ CONJUGATION — verbs ending in -ir follow another pattern
3ᴿᴰ CONJUGATION — verbs ending in -re follow another pattern

CONSULTING THE DICTIONARY

In English it is possible to change the meaning of a verb by placing short words (prepositions or adverbs) after it.

For example, the verb *look* in Column A below changes meaning depending on the word that follows it *(to, after, for, into)*. In French, it is impossible to change the meaning of a verb by adding a preposition or an adverb as in Column A. An entirely different French verb corresponds to each meaning.

COLUMN A		MEANING	FRENCH
to look	→	to look at	**regarder**
		I *looked at* the photo.	
to look *for*	→	to search for	**chercher**
		I *am looking for* a book.	
to look *after*	→	to take care of	**surveiller**
		I *am looking after* the children.	
to look *into*	→	to study	**étudier**
		We'll *look into* the problem.	

When consulting an English-French dictionary, all the examples under Column A can be found under the dictionary entry *look* (**regarder**); however, you will have to search under that entry for the specific expression *look for* (**chercher**), or *look after* (**surveiller**), to find the correct French equivalent.

Don't select the first entry under *look* and then add on the French equivalent for *after, for, into,* etc.; the result will be meaningless in French.

— *REVIEW* —

Circle the words that you would replace with an infinitive in French.

1. Mary has nothing more to do today.

2. The students must study their lessons.

3. Paul wants to learn French.

4. They can leave on Tuesday.

5. Paul and Mary hope to travel this summer.

WHAT IS A SUBJECT?

1   In a sentence the person or thing that performs
the action of the verb is called the **SUBJECT**.

To find the subject of a sentence, always look for the verb
first, then ask, *who?* or *what?* before the verb (see *What is a
Verb?*, p. 19). The answer will be the subject.[1]

> Paul speaks French.
> > Verb: speaks
> > Who speaks French? Answer: Paul.
> > *Paul* is the subject.
10 > > The subject is singular (see p. 9). It refers to one person.

> Paul's books cost a lot of money.
> > Verb: cost
> > What costs a lot of money? Answer: books.
> > *Books* is the subject.
> > The subject is plural. It refers to more than one thing.

If a sentence has more than one verb, you have to find
the subject of each verb.

> The ***boys* were** cooking, while ***Mary* set** the table.
> > *Boys* is the subject of *were* .
20 > > (Note that the subject is plural.)
> > *Mary* is the subject of *set*.
> > (Note that the subject is singular.)

IN ENGLISH——————————————————————

Always ask *who?* or *what?* before the verb to find the subject. Never assume that the first word in the sentence is
the subject. Subjects can be located in several different
places, as you can see in the following examples (the ***subject*** is in boldface and the *verb* italicized):

30 > Did **the game** *start* on time?
> After playing for two hours, **Paul** *became* exhausted.
> Mary's **brothers** *arrived* yesterday.

---

[1]The subject performs the action in an active sentence, but is acted upon in a passive
sentence (see *What is Meant by Active and Passive Voice?*, p. 160).

IN FRENCH ───────────────────────────────

The subject of a sentence is identified the same way as it is in English. Also, as in English, it can be located in different places in the sentence.

CAREFUL — In both English and French it is important to find the subject of each verb to make sure that the verb form agrees with the subject (see *What is a Verb Conjugation?*, p. 33).

40

— *REVIEW* —

Find the subjects in the sentences below.
- Next to Q, write the question you need to ask to find the subject of the sentences below.
- Next to A, write the answer to the question you just asked.
- Circle if the subject is singular (S) or plural (P).

1. When the bell rang, all the children ran out.

   Q: _____

   A: _____   S   P

   Q: _____

   A: _____   S   P

2. One waiter took the order and another brought the food.

   Q: _____

   A: _____   S   P

   Q: _____

   A: _____   S   P

3. The first-year students voted for the class president.

   Q: _____

   A: _____   S   P

4. French is a beautiful language, but it is difficult to learn.

   Q: _____

   A: _____   S   P

   Q: _____

   A: _____   S   P

CHAPTER

9

WHAT IS A PRONOUN?

A **PRONOUN** is a word used in place of one or more nouns.
It may stand, therefore, for a person, animal,
place, thing, event, or idea.

For instance, rather than repeating the proper noun "Paul" in the following two sentences, it can be replaced by a pronoun in the second sentence.

Paul likes to swim. *Paul* practices every day.
Paul likes to swim. *He* practices every day.

A pronoun can only be used to refer to someone (or something) that has already been mentioned. The word that the pronoun replaces or refers to is called the **ANTECEDENT** of the pronoun. In the example above, the pronoun *he* refers to the proper noun *Paul*. *Paul* is the antecedent of the pronoun *he*.

There are different types of pronouns, each serving a different function and following different rules. Listed below are the more important types and the chapters in which they are discussed.

PERSONAL PRONOUNS — These pronouns replace nouns referring to persons or things which have been previously mentioned. A different set of pronouns is often used depending on the pronoun's function in the sentence.

- as subject (see p. 28)

  I go; *they* read; *he* runs; *she* sings.

- as direct object (see p. 111)

  Paul loves *it*. Jane met *him*.

- as indirect object (see p. 111)

  Jane gave *us* the book. Speak to *them*.

- as object of a preposition (see p. 111)

  Paul is going out with *her*.

- as a disjunctive (see p. 119)

  Who is there? *Me*.

REFLEXIVE PRONOUNS — These pronouns refer back to the subject of the sentence (see p. 123).

> I cut *myself*. We washed *ourselves*. Mary dressed *herself*.

INTERROGATIVE PRONOUNS — These pronouns are used to ask questions (see p. 133).

> *Who* is that? *What* do you want?

DEMONSTRATIVE PRONOUNS — These pronouns are used to point out persons or things (see p. 155).

> *This (one)* is expensive. *That (one)* is cheap.

POSSESSIVE PRONOUNS — These pronouns are used to show possession (see p. 128).

> Whose book is that? *Mine. Yours* is on the table.

RELATIVE PRONOUNS — These pronouns are used to introduce relative clauses (see p. 141).

> The man *who* came is very nice.
> That is the book *which* you read last summer.

INDEFINITE PRONOUNS — These pronouns are used to refer to unidentified persons or things.

> *One* doesn't do that.
> *Something* is wrong.

French indefinite pronouns correspond in usage to their English equivalents. They can be studied in your textbook.

IN ENGLISH————————————————————————
Each type of pronoun follows a different set of rules.

IN FRENCH————————————————————————
As in English, each type of pronoun follows a different set of rules. Moreover, French pronouns usually correspond in gender and number with their antecedent.

— *REVIEW* —

Circle the pronouns in the sentences below.
- Draw an arrow from the pronoun to its antecedent, or antecedents if there is more than one.

1. Did Mary call Peter? Yes, she called him last night.

2. The coat and dress are elegant, but they are expensive.

3. Mary baked the cookies herself.

4. Paul and I are very tired. We went out last night.

5. Since the book is not on the table, it might be under it.

CHAPTER

10

WHAT IS A SUBJECT PRONOUN?

A **SUBJECT PRONOUN** is a pronoun used
as a subject of a verb.

He worked while *she* read.
Who worked? Answer: He.
He is the subject of the verb *worked*.

Who read? Answer: She.
She is the subject of the verb *read*.

Subject pronouns are divided into three groups: 1st, 2nd,
and 3rd person pronouns. The word **PERSON** in this instance
does not necessarily mean a human being; it is a grammatical term which can refer to any noun.

IN ENGLISH

Here is a list of subject pronouns.

1ST PERSON

I → the person speaking → SINGULAR
we → the person speaking plus others → PLURAL

Mary and I are free this evening. *We* are going out.

2ND PERSON

you → the person or persons spoken to → SINGULAR or PLURAL

Paul, do *you* sing folksongs?
Peter, Paul and Mary, do *you* sing folk songs?

3RD PERSON

he, she, it → the person or object spoken about → SINGULAR
they → the persons or objects spoken about → PLURAL

Mary and Paul are free this evening. *They* are going out.

IN FRENCH

French subject pronouns are also identified as 1st, 2nd and
3rd persons. They are usually divided into singular and
plural and presented in the following order:

SINGULAR

1ST PERSON	I	je
2ND PERSON	you	tu
3RD PERSON	he	il
	she	elle
	it	il or elle

PLURAL

1ST PERSON	we	**nous**	40
2ND PERSON	you	**vous**	
3RD PERSON	they	**ils** or **elles**	

As you can see above, there are three English subject pronouns which have more than one equivalent in French: *you* (**tu** or **vous**), *it* (**il** or **elle**) and *they* (**ils** or **elles**). Let us look at each of these pronouns.

———— "YOU" (2nd person singular and plural) ————

> **tu** (2nd person singular) or
> **vous** (2nd person plural)   50

IN ENGLISH

The same pronoun "you" is used to address one or more than one person.

> Mary, are *you* coming with me?
> Mary and Paul, are *you* coming with me?

The same pronoun "you" is used to address the President of the United States or your dog.

> Do *you* have any questions, Mr. President?
> *You* are a good dog, Heidi.   60

IN FRENCH

1. When you are addressing one person there are two forms, depending on the person and whether or not you are on familiar terms with him or her.

   - when speaking to a child, an animal, a family member, a friend, or anyone with whom you are on familiar terms, use the FAMILIAR FORM → "TU" (2nd person singular).

     > *Mom, are **you** coming with us?*   70
     > |
     > **tu**

   - when speaking to a person with whom you are not on familiar terms, use the FORMAL FORM or the POLITE FORM → "VOUS" (2nd person plural). Notice that even though the form is plural, it is used to address one person.

     > *Mrs. Smith, are **you** coming with us?*
     > |
     > **vous**
     >   80

When you are speaking to an adult and unsure which form to use, use **vous**.

2. When you are addressing more than one person whether you are on familiar terms with them or not, there is only one form, "vous" (2nd person plural).

Mom and Dad, are you coming with us?

vous

Mr. and Mrs. Smith, are you coming with us?

vous

─────────── **"IT"** (3rd person singular) ───────────

il (3rd person singular masculine) or
elle (3rd person singular feminine)

IN ENGLISH

Whenever you are speaking about one thing or idea, you use the pronoun *it*.

Where is the book? *It* is on the table.
Here is the chair. *It* is comfortable.

IN FRENCH

The subject pronoun used to refer to a thing or an idea depends on the gender of its **ANTECEDENT**, that is, the noun it replaces.

- masculine antecedent → **il**

Où est le livre? **Il** est sur la table.

masc. sing.   masc. sing.
antecedent   pronoun

*Where is the book? **It** is on the table.*

- feminine antecedent → **elle**

Voici la chaise. **Elle** est confortable.

fem. sing.   fem. sing.
antecedent   pronoun

*Here is the chair. **It** is comfortable.*

─────────── **"THEY"** (3rd person plural) ───────────

ils (3rd person plural masculine) or
elles (3rd person plural feminine)

IN ENGLISH

Whenever you are speaking about more than one person or object, you use the plural pronoun *they*.

Paul and Henry are students; *they* study a lot.
Where are the books? *They* are on the table.

IN FRENCH

The subject pronoun used depends on the gender of the noun *they* replaces; i.e. the French pronoun must agree with the gender of the antecedent.

- masculine antecedent → **ils**   130

>   Où sont les livres? **Ils** sont sur la table.
> | |
>   masc. pl.   masc. pl.
>   antecedent   pronoun
>   *Where are the books? **They** are on the table.*

>   Paul et Henri sont étudiants; **ils** étudient beaucoup.
> |_____| |
>   masc. sing.   masc. pl.
>   antecedents   pronoun
>   *Paul and Henry are students. **They** study a lot.*

>   Où sont le livre et le cahier? **Ils** sont sur la table.   140
> |_____| |
>   masc. sing.   masc. pl.
>   antecedents   pronoun
>   *Where are the book and the notebook? **They** are on the table.*

- feminine antecedent → **elles**

>   Voici les chaises; **elles** sont confortables.
> | |
>   fem. pl.   fem. pl.
>   antecedent   pronoun
>   *Here are the chairs; **they** are comfortable.*

>   Anne et Marie sont étudiantes; **elles** étudient beaucoup.   150
> |_____| |
>   fem. sing.   fem. pl.
>   antecedents   pronoun
>   *Anne and Mary are students. **They** study a lot.*

>   Où sont la clé et la montre? **Elles** sont sur la table.
> |_____| |
>   fem. sing.   fem. pl.
>   antecedents   pronoun
>   *Where are the key and the watch? **They** are on the table.*

- antecedents of different genders → **ils**

>   Voici la clé et le cahier. **Ils** sont sur la table.   160
> | | |
>   fem. sing. + masc. sing. masc. pl.
> |_ antecedents _| pronoun
>   *Here are the key and the notebook. **They** are on the table.*

— *REVIEW* —

Write the French subject pronoun that you would use to replace the words in italics.

■ Write the corresponding person and number of each pronoun.

	FRENCH SUBJECT PRONOUN	PERSON	NUMBER
1. Am *I* invited?	_____	_____	_____
2. Come on children, *you* must go to bed now.	_____	_____	_____
3. *Paul and I* are going out.	_____	_____	_____
4. Mommy, *you* have to give me a kiss.	_____	_____	_____
5. *Mary and Helen* are home.	_____	_____	_____
6. Do *you and your wife* like sports?	_____	_____	_____
7. *My brother and sister* speak French.	_____	_____	_____

WHAT IS A VERB CONJUGATION?

A VERB CONJUGATION is a list of the six possible forms of the   1
verb for a particular tense. For each tense, there is
one verb form for each of the pronouns
used as the subject of the verb.

> I am
> you are
> he, she, it is
> we are
> you are
> they are
                                                                       10

Different tenses have different verb forms, but the princi-
ple of conjugation remains the same. In this chapter all
our examples are in the present tense.

IN ENGLISH

The verb *to be* conjugated above is the English verb which
changes the most; it has three forms: *am, are,* and *is.* (In
conversation the initial vowel is often replaced by an
apostrophe: *I'm, you're, he's.*) Other English verbs only
have two forms. Let us look at the verb *to sing* .
                                                                       20

SINGULAR

1ST PERSON	I *sing*
2ND PERSON	you *sing*
3RD PERSON	he *sings*
	she *sings*
	it *sings*

PLURAL

1ST PERSON	we *sing*
2ND PERSON	you *sing*
3RD PERSON	they *sing*

Because English verbs change so little, it isn't necessary   30
to learn "to conjugate a verb"; that is, to list all its possible
forms. For most verbs, it is much simpler to say that the
verb adds an "-s" in the 3rd person singular.

IN FRENCH

Unlike English, French verb forms change from one person to another so that when you learn a new verb, you
must also learn how to conjugate it. First, you must establish whether the verb is regular or irregular.

- Verbs whose forms follow a pattern are called REGULAR VERBS. Only one example must be memorized and the pattern can then be applied to other verbs in the same group.
- Verbs whose forms do not follow a pattern are called IRREGULAR VERBS. The conjugation of these verbs must be memorized individually.

The conjugation of a verb, whether regular or irregular, is made up of a pronoun subject and the verb form that goes with that subject.

─────────── CHOOSING THE PROPER "PERSON" (see p. 28) ───────────

Below is the conjugation of the regular verb **chanter** *(to sing)*. Notice that each of the six persons has its own ending and that different pronouns belonging to the same person have the same verb form. For instance, the 3ʳᵈ person singular has two pronouns, **il** and **elle**, but they both have the same verb form: **chante**.

SINGULAR

1ˢᵀ PERSON	je chante	*I sing*
2ᴺᴰ PERSON	tu chantes	*you sing*
3ᴿᴰ PERSON {	il chante	*he sings, it sings*
	elle chante	*she sings, it sings*

PLURAL

1ˢᵀ PERSON	nous chantons	*we sing*
2ᴺᴰ PERSON	vous chantez	*you sing*
3ᴿᴰ PERSON {	ils chantent	*they sing*
	elles chantent	*they sing*

To choose the proper verb form, it is important to identify the person (1ˢᵗ, 2ⁿᵈ or 3ʳᵈ) and the number (singular or plural) of the subject.

1ˢᵀ PERSON SINGULAR — The subject is always **je** *(I)*.

Le matin **je chante** bien.
*In the morning **I sing** well.*

2ᴺᴰ PERSON SINGULAR — The subject is always **tu** *(you)*.

Jean, **tu chantes** bien.
*John, **you sing** well.*

3ʳᴰ PERSON SINGULAR — The subject can be expressed in one of three ways:

80

1. the 3ʳᵈ person singular masculine pronoun **il** *(he, it)* or the 3ʳᵈ person singular feminine pronoun **elle** *(she, it)*

> **Il chante** bien.
> *He sings well.*

> Regardez ce livre. **Il est** intéressant.
> *Look at this book. It is interesting.*

> **Elle chante** bien.
> *She sings well.*

90

> Voici la chaise. **Elle est** confortable.
> *Here is the chair. It is comfortable.*

2. a proper noun

> **Marie chante** bien.
> feminine → **elle**
> *Mary sings well.*

> **Paul chante** bien.
> masculine → **il**
> *Paul sings well.*

100

In both these sentences the proper noun could be replaced by the pronoun *she* (**elle** → fem.) or *he* (**il** → masc.) so that you must use the 3ʳᵈ person singular form of the verb.

3. a singular common noun

> **La fille chante** bien.
> feminine → **elle**
> *The girl sings well.*

> **L'oiseau chante** bien.
> masculine → **il**
> *The bird sings well.*

110

In both these sentences the common noun could be replaced by the pronoun *she* (**elle** → fem.) or *it* (**il** → masc.) so that you must use the 3ʳᵈ person singular form of the verb.

1ˢᵀ PERSON PLURAL — The subject can be expressed in one of two ways:

1. the first person plural pronoun **nous** *(we)*

> **Nous chantons** bien.
> *We sing well.*

120

2. a multiple subject in which the speaker is included

Marie, Paul et moi chantons bien.
nous

Mary, Paul and I sing well.

The subject, *Mary, Paul* and *I*, could be replaced by the pronoun *we*, so that you must use the 1st person plural form of the verb.

2ND PERSON PLURAL — The subject is always **vous** *(you).*

Madame Dupont, **vous chantez** bien.
Mrs. Dupont, you sing well.

3RD PERSON PLURAL — The subject can be expressed in one of three ways:

1. The 3rd person plural masculine pronoun **ils** *(they)* or the 3rd person plural feminine pronoun **elles** *(they)*

Ils chantent bien.
They sing well.

Regardez ces livres. **Ils sont** intéressants.
*Look at these books. **They are** interesting.*

Elles chantent bien.
They sing well.

Voici les chaises. **Elles sont** confortables.
*Here are the chairs. **They are** comfortable.*

2. two or more proper or common nouns

Marie et Paul chantent bien.
feminine + masculine → **ils**
Mary and Paul sing well.

La fille et le garçon chantent bien.
feminine + masculine → **ils**
The girl and the boy sing well.

3. a plural noun

Les filles chantent bien.
feminine pl. → **elles**
The girls sing well.

──────────── **HOW TO CONJUGATE A VERB** ────────────

A French verb, whether regular or irregular, is composed of two parts:

1. the STEM, "LA RACINE" in French, is found by dropping the last two letters from the infinitive (see *What is the Infinitive?*, p. 21).

INFINITIVE	STEM
chanter	chant-
finir	fin-
vendre	vend-

In regular verbs the stem usually remains the same throughout a conjugation. The stem may change in irregular verbs.

2. the ENDING, "LA TERMINAISON" in French, changes for each person in the conjugation of regular and irregular verbs.

Regular verbs are divided into three GROUPS, also called CONJUGATIONS, identified by the infinitive ending of the verb.

-er	-ir	-re
1st group	2nd group	3rd group

Each of the three verb groups has its own set of endings for each tense (see *What is Meant by Tense?*, p. 49). Memorizing the conjugation of one sample verb for each group enables you to conjugate all the other regular verbs belonging to that group.

As an example of the steps to follow to conjugate a regular verb, let us look at verbs of the 1st group (-**er** verbs); that is, verbs like **parler** (*to speak*) and **aimer** (*to love*) that follow the pattern of **chanter** (*to sing*) conjugated above.

1. Identify the group of the verb by its infinitive ending.

parler
aimer   →1st conjugation or group

2. Find the verb stem by removing the infinitive ending.

parl-
aim-

3. Add the ending that agrees with the subject.

je parle	j'aime
tu parles	tu aimes
il parle	il aime
elle parle	elle aime

nous parlons	nous aimons
vous parlez	vous aimez
ils parlent	ils aiment
elles parlent	elles aiment

The endings of regular verbs belonging to the other groups are different, but the process of conjugation is the same. Just follow the three steps above.

As irregular verbs are introduced in your textbook, their entire conjugation will be given so that you can memorize them individually. Be sure to do so because many common verbs are irregular (**avoir**, *to have*; **être**, *to be*; **aller**, *to go*; and **faire**, *to make*, for example).

CAREFUL — French verb forms are often pronounced the same way, but written differently. Therefore, the only way to write the proper ending of a verb is to identify its subject. This is particularly true of verbs of the 1ˢᵗ group where, for instance, *parle, parles, parlent* have an identical pronunciation *(parle)*, but have different spellings depending on their subject.

— *REVIEW* —

Write the stem and conjugate the regular verb **porter** *(to carry, to wear)*.

STEM: _____

je _____   nous_____

tu_____   vous _____

il/elle_____   ils/elles _____

12

WHAT ARE AUXILIARY VERBS?

A verb is called an AUXILIARY VERB or HELPING VERB when
it helps another verb, called the MAIN VERB,
form one of its tenses.

He *has been* gone two weeks. | *has* | AUXILIARY VERB
| *been* | AUXILIARY VERB
| *gone* | MAIN VERB

IN ENGLISH ————————————————————————

There are three auxiliary verbs, *to have, to be*, and *to do*,
as well as a series of auxiliary words such as *will, would,*
may, must, can, could, which are used to change the
tense and meaning of the main verb.

- Auxiliaries are used primarily to indicate the tense of
the main verb (present, past, future — see *What is Meant*
by Tense?, p. 49).

  Mary *is reading* a book. PRESENT
  auxiliary *to be*

  Mary *has read* a book. PAST
  auxiliary *to have*

  Mary *will read* a book. FUTURE
  auxiliary *will*

- The auxiliary verb *to do* is used to help formulate questions and to make sentences negative (see *What are*
Declarative and Interrogative Sentences?, p. 45 and *What*
are Affirmative and Negative Sentences?, p. 42).

  Does Mary *read* a book? INTERROGATIVE SENTENCE
  Mary *does not* read a book. NEGATIVE SENTENCE

IN FRENCH ————————————————————————

There are only two auxiliary verbs: **avoir** (*to have*) and **être**
(*to be*). They are used to change the tense of the main
verb.

The other English auxiliaries such as *do, does, did, will* or
would do not exist as auxiliaries in French. Their meaning

is conveyed either by a different structure or by a form of the main verb. You will find more on this subject under the chapters dealing with the different tenses.

The verbs **avoir** and **être** are irregular verbs whose conjugations must be memorized. They are important verbs because they serve both as auxiliary verbs and main verbs.

J'**ai** un livre.	avoir *(to have)*	MAIN VERB
*I **have** a book.*		
J'**ai** lu un livre.	**avoir**	AUXILIARY VERB
*I **have** read a book.*	lire *(to read)*	MAIN VERB
Je **suis** à la maison.	être *(to be)*	MAIN VERB
*I **am** at home.*		
Je **suis** allé à la maison.	**être**	AUXILIARY VERB
*I **have** gone home.*	aller *(to go)*	MAIN VERB

A verb tense composed of an auxiliary verb plus a main verb is called a **COMPOUND TENSE**, as opposed to a **SIMPLE TENSE** which is a tense composed of only the main verb.

Je **mange**.
simple tense
present of **manger**
I eat.

J'**ai mangé**.
auxiliary main
verb   verb
compound tense
past tense of **manger**
I have eaten.

─────── **AUXILIARY VERBS ARE USED TO INDICATE TENSE** ───────

Verbs take either **avoir** or **être** as auxiliary to form all of their compound tenses (see p. 57 for guidelines on selecting the proper auxiliary). The auxiliary, conjugated in the different tenses, and the past participle of the main verb (see *What is a Participle?*, p. 53) form the various tenses of the main verb.

Let us look at examples of some compound tenses. The first sentence of each pair is a verb which takes a form of **avoir** as auxiliary (**manger**, *to eat)* and the second a verb which takes a form of **être** as auxiliary (**aller** *(to go)*.

PASSÉ COMPOSÉ (PERFECT) — Present of **avoir** or **être** + past participle of main verb (see *What is the Past Tense?*, p. 56). Notice that there are two possible English equivalents.

Le garçon **a mangé** la pomme.
*The boy **ate (has eaten)** the apple.*

La fille **est allée** au cinéma.
*The girl **went (has gone)** to the movies.*

PLUS-QUE-PARFAIT (PLUPERFECT) — Imperfect of **avoir** or **être** + past participle of main verb (see *What is the Pluperfect Tense?*, p. 61).

Le garçon **avait mangé** la pomme.
*The boy **had eaten** the apple.*

La fille **était allée** au cinéma.
*The girl **had gone** to the movies.*

FUTUR ANTÉRIEUR (FUTURE PERFECT) — Future of **avoir** or **être** + past participle of main verb (see *What is the Future Perfect Tense?*, p. 67).

Le garçon **aura mangé** la pomme.
*The boy **will have eaten** the apple.*

La fille **sera allée** au cinéma.
*The girl **will have gone** to the movies.*

CONDITIONNEL PASSÉ (PAST CONDITIONAL) — Conditional of **avoir** or **être** + past participle of main verb (see p. 75 in *What is the Conditional?*).

Le garçon **aurait mangé** la pomme.
*The boy **would have eaten** the apple.*

La fille **serait allée** au cinéma.
*The girl **would have gone** to the movies.*

You will learn other compound tenses as your study of French progresses.

— REVIEW —

Cross out the English auxiliary verbs which are not used as auxiliaries in French.

1. Did the children do their homework?

2. They will do their homework tomorrow.

3. Do you want to study now?

4. Have the children done their homework?

CHAPTER

13

WHAT ARE AFFIRMATIVE AND NEGATIVE SENTENCES?

A sentence can be classified according
to whether or not the verb is negated,
that is, made negative with the word *not*.

An **AFFIRMATIVE SENTENCE** is a sentence whose verb is not negated. It states a fact that is.

> France is a country in Europe.
> Paul will work at the university.
> They liked to travel.

A **NEGATIVE SENTENCE** is a sentence whose verb is negated with the word ***not***. It states a fact that is not.

> France is *not* a country in Asia.
> Paul will *not* work at the university.
> They *did not* like to travel.

IN ENGLISH

An affirmative sentence can be made negative in one of two ways:

1. by adding ***not*** after auxiliary verbs or auxiliary words (see *What are Auxiliary Verbs?*, p. 39)

AFFIRMATIVE	NEGATIVE
Paul *is* a student.	Paul is *not* a student.
Mary *can* do it.	Mary can*not* do it.
They *will* travel.	They will *not* travel.

Frequently, the word *not* is attached to the verb and the letter "o" is replaced by an apostrophe; this is called a **CONTRACTION**: is not → isn't; cannot → can't; will not → won't.

2. by adding the auxiliary verb ***do, does***, or ***did + not +*** the dictionary form of the main verb (*do* or *does* is used for negatives in the present tense and *did* for negatives in the past tense—see *What is the Present Tense?*, p. 51 and *What is the Past Tense?*, p. 56)

AFFIRMATIVE	NEGATIVE
We *study* a lot.	We *do not* study a lot.
Mary *writes* well.	Mary *does not* write well.
The train *arrived*.	The train *did not* arrive.

Frequently, *do, does,* or *did* is contracted with *not:* do not → don't; does not → doesn't; did not → didn't.

IN FRENCH

The basic rule for turning an affirmative sentence into a negative sentence is to put **ne** right after the subject and the negative word **pas** *(not)* after the conjugated verb. (If the conjugated verb starts with a vowel, **ne** changes to **n'**.)

AFFIRMATIVE	**NEGATIVE**
Elles **mangent** beaucoup.	Elles **ne** mangent **pas** beaucoup.
*They **eat** a lot.*	conjugated verb
	*They **do not** eat a lot.*

Marie **écrit** bien.   Marie **n'**écrit **pas** bien.
*Mary **writes** well.*   conjugated verb
                        *Mary **does not** write well.*

Le train **est** arrivé.   Le train **n'**est **pas** arrivé.
*The train **has** arrived.*   conjugated verb
                        *The train has **not** arrived.*

CAREFUL — Remember that there is no equivalent for the auxiliary words *do, does, did* in French; do not try to include them in negative sentences.

NEGATIVE WORDS

In both English and French there are negative words that can be added to an affirmative sentence.

IN ENGLISH

The most common negative words are: *nothing, nobody, no one, never.*

> I have *nothing* to give you.
> He *never* arrives on time.
> Before his exam he sees *no one (nobody).*

IN FRENCH

The most common negative words are: **rien** *(nothing)*, **jamais** *(never)*, and **personne** *(nobody, no one)*. They are always used with **ne**.

> Je **n'**ai **rien** à vous donner.
> *I have **nothing** to give you.*

Il **n'**arrive **jamais** à l'heure.
*He **never** arrives on time.*

Avant son examen, il **ne** voit **personne**.
*Before his exam he sees **no one (nobody)**.*

The position of **ne** and the negative word changes depending on the negative word and its function in the sentence. Consult your French textbook.

— *REVIEW* —

Write the negative of each sentence.
- Circle the words which indicate the negative in the sentences you have just written.
- Box in the English words around which you would place the **ne . . . pas** in a French sentence.

1. We want to speak English in class.

   _____

2. He does his homework.

   _____

3. Helen was home this morning.

   _____

4. Paul can go to the restaurant with us.

   _____

WHAT ARE DECLARATIVE AND INTERROGATIVE SENTENCES?

A sentence can be classified as to whether it is making a statement or asking a question.

A **DECLARATIVE SENTENCE** is a sentence that makes a statement.

Columbus discovered America in 1492.

An **INTERROGATIVE SENTENCE** is a sentence that asks a question.

Did Columbus discover America in 1492?

In written language, an interrogative sentence always ends with a question mark.

IN ENGLISH

A declarative sentence can be changed to an interrogative sentence in one of two ways:

1. by adding the auxiliary verb **do, does,** or **did** before the subject and changing the main verb to the dictionary form of the verb (*do* and *does* are used to introduce a question in the present tense and *did* to introduce a question in the past tense — see *What is the Present Tense?*, p. 51 and *What is the Past Tense?*, p. 56)

DECLARATIVE SENTENCE	**INTERROGATIVE SENTENCE**
Philip *likes* the class.	*Does* Philip *like* the class?
present 3rd pers. sing.	present 3rd pers. sing. + dictionary form
Paul and Mary *sing* well.	*Do* Paul and Mary *sing* well?
present 3rd pers. pl.	present 3rd pers. pl. + dictionary form
Alice *went* to Paris.	*Did* Alice *go* to Paris?
past	past + dictionary form

2. by inverting the normal word order of subject + verb to verb + subject. This **INVERSION** process can only be used with auxiliary verbs or auxiliary words (see *What are Auxiliary Verbs?*, p. 39).

DECLARATIVE SENTENCE	INTERROGATIVE SENTENCE
Paul is home.	*Is Paul home?*
subject + verb "to be"	verb + subject
You have received a letter.	*Have you received a letter?*
subject + "to have" + main verb	"to have" + subject + main verb
She will come tomorrow.	*Will she come tomorrow?*
subject + *will* + main verb	*will* + subject + main verb

IN FRENCH

A declarative sentence can be changed to an interrogative sentence in one of two ways:

1. by adding the expression **est-ce que** before the statement

> Vous mangez à la maison ce soir.
> **Est-ce que** vous mangez à la maison ce soir?
> *You are eating at home this evening.*
> *Are you eating at home this evening?*

> Paul mange à la maison.
> **Est-ce que** Paul mange à la maison?
> *Paul eats at home.*
> *Does Paul eat at home?*

> Je peux manger maintenant.
> **Est-ce que** je peux manger maintenant?
> *I can eat now.*
> *May I eat now?*

2. by using the inversion form; that is, by putting any pronoun subject, except **je**, after the verb. (If **je** is the subject, always use the **est-ce que** form.)

- when the subject is a pronoun, simply invert the verb and pronoun subject

> Vous mangez à la maison ce soir.
> **Mangez-vous** à la maison ce soir?
> *You are eating at home this evening.*
> ***Are you eating** at home this evening?*

- when the subject is a noun, follow these steps:
  1. State the noun subject.
  2. State the verb and, when writing, add a hyphen.
  3. State the subject pronoun that corresponds to the gender and number of the subject (see p. 28).

Let's look at a few examples.

> Paul est à la maison.
> **Paul** est-**il** à la maison?
> (word-for-word: *Paul* is *he* home)
> *Paul is home.*
> *Is Paul home?*

80

> La montre et la clé sont sur la table.
> **La montre et la clé** sont-**elles** sur la table?
> (word-for-word: *the watch and the key* are *they* on the table)
> > Since both subjects (**la montre** and **la clé**) are femi-
> > nine, the pronoun will be feminine plural → **elles**.
> *The watch and the key are on the table.*
> *Are the watch and the key on the table?*

90

> Paul et Marie chantent ensemble.
> **Paul et Marie** chantent-**ils** ensemble?
> (word-for-word: *Paul and Mary* do *they* sing together)
> > Since one subject is masculine (**Paul**) and the other
> > feminine (**Marie**), the pronoun will be masculine
> > plural → **ils** (see p. 31).
> *Paul and Mary sing together.*
> *Do Paul and Mary sing together?*

The interrogative form of the 3rd person singular of verbs of the 1st conjugation is irregular. Make sure to consult your textbook.

100

CAREFUL — When *do, does,* or *did* are used as auxiliaries make sure that you do not translate them. In the interrogative, just like **est-ce que**, they signal a question.

────────── **TAG QUESTIONS** ──────────

In both English and French when you expect a yes-or-no answer, you can also transform a statement into a question by adding a short phrase at the end of the statement. This short phrase is called a **TAG**.

110

IN ENGLISH

There are many different tags, depending on factors such as the tense of the verb of the statement and whether the statement is affirmative or negative. For instance, affirmative statements take negative tags and negative statements take affirmative tags.

> Paul and Mary *sing* together, *don't they?*
> Paul and Mary *don't sing* together, *do they?*

120   **IN FRENCH**

There is only one tag, **n'est-ce pas?** It can be added to any statement requiring a yes-or-no answer to turn it into a question.

Paul et Mary chantent ensemble, n'est-ce pas?
*Paul and Mary sing together, **don't they?***

Paul et Mary ne chantent pas ensemble, n'est-ce pas?
*Paul and Mary don't sing together, **do they?***

— *REVIEW* —

I. Write the interrogative form for each of the sentences below.
- Circle the words which indicate the interrogative in the sentences you have just written.

1. Paul and Mary studied all evening.

_____

2. His brother eats a lot.

_____

3. The girl's parents speak French.

_____

II. Let us see the different ways the declarative sentence below can be changed to an interrogative sentence in French.

My mother and father went to the movies.

1. Box in the word before which you would place **est-ce que?**
2. Circle the word after which you would place **n'est-ce pas?**
3. To use the inversion form, fill in the answers to the steps below.
4. In the space provided, fill in the answer in French.

- State the noun subject: _____

- State the verb: _____

- State the pronoun that
  corresponds to the subject: ____ → IN FRENCH: ____

WHAT IS MEANT BY TENSE?

The TENSE of a verb indicates when the action of the verb [1]
takes place: at the present time, in the past, or in the
future. The word *tense* comes from the same word
as the French word "temps," which means *time*.

I am eating.	PRESENT
I ate.	PAST
I shall eat.	FUTURE

As you can see in the above examples, just by putting
the verb in a different tense and without giving any addi- [10]
tional information (such as "I am eating *now*," "I ate *yesterday*," "I shall eat *tomorrow*"), you can indicate when the
action of the verb takes place.

Tenses may be classified according to the way they are
formed. A SIMPLE TENSE consists of only one verb form (I
ate), while a COMPOUND TENSE consists of one or more auxiliaries plus the main verb (I *am eating*).

In this section we will only consider tenses of the
indicative mood (see *What is Meant by Mood?*, p. 69).

IN ENGLISH———————————————————————— [20]

Listed below are the main tenses of the indicative mood
whose equivalents you will encounter in French:

PRESENT

I study	PRESENT
I do study	PRESENT EMPHATIC
I am studying	PRESENT CONTINUOUS

PAST

I studied	SIMPLE PAST (PAST DEFINITE)
I did study	PAST EMPHATIC [30]
I have studied	PERFECT
I had studied	PLUPERFECT
I was studying	PAST CONTINUOUS

FUTURE

I shall study	FUTURE
I shall have studied	FUTURE PERFECT

As you can see, there are only two simple tenses (present and simple past), all of the other tenses are compound tenses.

IN FRENCH ────────────────────────────────────

Listed below are the main tenses of the indicative mood that you will encounter in French:

PRESENT

j'étudie	*I study, I do study*	PRÉSENT (PRESENT)
	I am studying	

PAST

j'étudiais	*I was studying*	IMPARFAIT (IMPERFECT)
j'ai étudié	*I have studied*	PASSÉ COMPOSÉ (PERFECT)
	I did study	
j'avais étudié	*I had studied*	PLUS-QUE-PARFAIT (PLUPERFECT)

FUTURE

j'étudierai	*I shall study*	FUTUR (FUTURE)
j'aurai étudié	*I shall have studied*	FUTUR ANTÉRIEUR (FUTURE PERFECT)

As you can see, there are more simple tenses than in English (present, imperfect, future). The compound tenses in French are formed with the auxiliary verbs **avoir** or **être** + the past participle of the main verb. (The verb **étudier** above uses the auxiliary verb **avoir** to form its compound tenses.)

This handbook discusses the various tenses and their usage in separate chapters: *What is the Present Tense?*, p. 51; *What is the Past Tense?*, p. 56; *What is the Pluperfect Tense?*, p.61; *What is the Future Tense?*, p. 64; and *What is the Future Perfect Tense?*, p. 67. Verb tenses can be grouped according to the mood to which they belong (see *What is Meant by Mood?*, p. 69).

CAREFUL — Do not assume that tenses with the same name are used in the same way in English and in French.

WHAT IS THE PRESENT TENSE?

The PRESENT TENSE indicates that the action is happening at the present time. It can be at the moment the speaker is speaking, a habitual action, or a general truth.

> I *see* you.
> He *smokes* constantly.
> The sun *rises* every day.

IN ENGLISH

There are three forms of the verb which indicate the present tense. Each form has a slightly different meaning:

Mary *studies* in the library.	PRESENT
Mary *is studying* in the library.	PRESENT CONTINUOUS
Mary *does study* in the library.	PRESENT EMPHATIC

Depending on the way a question is worded, you will automatically choose one of the three above forms.

> Where does Mary study? She *studies* in the library.
> Where is Mary now? She *is studying* in the library.
> Does Mary study in the library? Yes, she *does [study* in the library].

IN FRENCH

The present tense, LE PRÉSENT in French, is a simple tense formed by adding a set of endings to the stem of the verb (see *What is a Verb Conjugation?*, p. 33). Your textbook will give you the present tense endings.

Unlike English, there is only one verb form to indicate the present tense. The French present tense is used to express the meaning of the English present, present continuous, and present emphatic tenses.

> *Mary **studies** in the library.*
> **étudie**
>
> *Mary **is studying** in the library.*
> **étudie**
>
> *Mary **does study** in the library.*
> **étudie**

40

CAREFUL — Since the present is always indicated by the ending of the verb, without an auxiliary verb such as *is* and *does,* you must not translate these English auxiliary verbs. Simply put the main verb in the present tense.

— *R E V I E W* —

Fill in the proper form of the verb *to read* in the following answers.
■ Write the French verb form for sentences 2, 3 and 4.

1. What does Mary do all day?

   She _____.

   FRENCH VERB: **lit.**

2. What is Mary doing now?

   She_____.

   FRENCH VERB: _____

3. Does Mary read French?

   Yes, she_____French.

   FRENCH VERB: _____

4. Has she read *The Red and the Black?*

   No, but, she_____ it right now.

   FRENCH VERB: _____

WHAT IS A PARTICIPLE?

A **PARTICIPLE** is a form of a verb which can be used [1]
in one of two ways: with an auxiliary verb to indicate
certain tenses, or as an adjective to describe something.

He *has closed* the door.

auxiliary + participle → past tense

He heard me through the *closed* door.

participle describing *door* → adjective

There are two types of participle: the present participle [10]
and the past participle.

─────────────── **PRESENT PARTICIPLE** ───────────────

IN ENGLISH

The present participle is easy to recognize because it is the
-ing form of the verb: *working, studying, dancing, playing*.

The present participle has two primary uses:

1. as the main verb in compound tenses with the auxiliary
   verb *to be* (see *What are Auxiliary Verbs?*, p. 39)

   She *is writing* with her new pen. [20]

   present continuous of *to write*

   They *were sleeping*.

   past continuous of *to sleep*

2. as an adjective (see *What is an Adjective?*, p. 80)

   The pen is a *writing* instrument.

   describes the noun *instrument*

   He woke the *sleeping* child.

   describes the noun *child* [30]

IN FRENCH

The present participle, **LE PARTICIPE PRÉSENT** in French, is
formed by adding -**ant** to the stem of the **nous**-form of
the present tense: chant~~ons~~ → chant**ant** *(singing)*, finis-
s~~ons~~ → finiss**ant** *(finishing)*.

The present participle is used differently and less frequently in French than in English. Refer to your textbook.

CAREFUL — Remember that the French equivalent of the English tenses formed with an auxiliary + present participle (*she is singing, they were dancing*) do not use participles in French. These English constructions correspond to a simple tense of the French verb.

*She **is singing**.*	→	Elle **chante**.
present continuous		present (see p. 51)
*They **were dancing**.*	→	Ils **dansaient**.
past continuous		imperfect (see p. 58)
*He **will be staying** here.*	→	Il **restera** ici.
future continuous		future (see p. 64)

PAST PARTICIPLE

IN ENGLISH

The past participle is formed in several ways. It is the form of the verb that follows *I have*: *I have **spoken**, I have **written**, I have **walked**.*

The past participle has two primary uses:

1. as the main verb in compound tenses with the auxiliary verb *to have*

> I *have **written*** all that I have to say.
> He *hasn't **spoken*** to me since our quarrel.

2. as an adjective

> Is the *written* word more important than the *spoken* word?
> describes the noun *word*   describes the noun *word*

IN FRENCH

The past participle, LE PARTICIPE PASSÉ in French, can be regular or irregular. Here are the endings of regular verbs:

- **-er** verbs add **-é** to the stem
- **-ir** verbs add **-i** to the stem
- **-re** verbs add **-u** to the stem

INFINITIVE	STEM	PAST PARTICIPLE
chanter	chant-	chanté
finir	fin-	fini
répondre	répond-	répondu

You will have to memorize irregular past participles individually. As you can see in the examples below, they can be very different from the infinitive.

INFINITIVE	PAST PARTICIPLE
être	été
avoir	eu
lire	lu
comprendre	compris
écrire	écrit

As in English, the past participle can be used as the main verb of a compound tense or as an adjective.

1. as the main verb in compound tenses with the auxiliary **avoir** *(to have)* or **être** *(to be)*

> Nous avons **compris** la leçon.
> *We have **understood** the lesson.*
>
> Paul est **allé** à la maison.
> *Paul has **gone** home.*

Many tenses are formed with the auxiliary verbs **avoir** or **être** + the past participle of the main verb (see p. 39-41). These tenses are discussed in various chapters of this handbook.

2. as an adjective which agrees with the noun it modifies in gender and number

> the *spoken language*
> la langue **parlée**
>
> > *Spoken* modifies the noun *language*. Since **la langue** *(language)* is feminine singular, the word for *spoken* must be feminine singular. This is shown by adding an -e to **parlé**.
>
> the **written** *words*
> les mots **écrits**
>
> > *Written* modifies the noun *words*. Since **les mots** *(words)* is masculine plural, the word for *written* must be masculine plural. This is shown by adding an -s to **écrit**.

— REVIEW —

Circle the auxiliary + present participles in the sentences below which are the equivalent of a simple tense in French.

1. I am speaking French.

2. Paul and Mary were studying for the exam.

3. Are you bringing the book to class ?

4. The students will be trying to memorize the verbs.

CHAPTER

18

WHAT IS THE PAST TENSE?

The PAST TENSE is used to express an action
that occurred in the past.

I *saw* you yesterday.

IN ENGLISH

There are several verb forms that indicate the action took
place in the past.[1]

I worked	SIMPLE PAST (PAST DEFINITE)
I have worked	PERFECT
I was working	PAST CONTINUOUS
I used to work	WITH HELPING VERB USED TO
I did work	PAST EMPHATIC

The simple past is called "simple" because it is a simple
tense; that is, it consists of one word (*worked* in the example above). The other past tenses are compound tenses;
that is, they consist of more than one word, an auxiliary
plus a main verb (*was working, did work*).

IN FRENCH

There are two French tenses which correspond to all the
English past verbal forms listed above: LE PASSÉ COMPOSÉ
and L'IMPARFAIT. We'll refer to these two tenses by their
French names because their usage does not correspond to
a specific English tense.

LE PASSÉ COMPOSÉ (PERFECT)

The **passé composé** is formed with the auxiliary verb
avoir *(to have)* or **être** *(to be)* conjugated in the present
tense + the past participle of the main verb (see *What are
Auxiliary Verbs?*, p. 39 and *What is a Participle?*, p. 53). As

in English, the past participle does not change form from
one person to another.

j'ai parlé	*I spoke, I have spoken*
avoir past participle auxiliary	
nous avons parlé	*we spoke, we have spoken*

---

[1]A separate section is devoted to the pluperfect *(I had worked)*, see p. 61.

je suis allé   *I went, I have gone*
  | |
être   past participle
auxiliary

il est allé   *he went, he has gone*

──────── SELECTION OF THE AUXILIARY AVOIR OR ÊTRE ────────

Most verbs use the auxiliary **avoir**. Therefore, it is easier for you to memorize the list of verbs conjugated with **être** and assume that all the other verbs are conjugated with **avoir**.

There are approximately sixteen common verbs, sometimes referred to by grammar books as "verbs of motion," that are conjugated with **être**. "Verbs of motion" is not an accurate description of these verbs since some of them, such as **rester** *(to stay, to remain)*, do not imply motion. You will find common "être verbs" easy to memorize in pairs of opposites:

aller	*to go*	≠	venir	*to come*
retourner	*to return*	≠	rester	*to remain*
entrer	*to come in*	≠	sortir	*to go out*
arriver	*to arrive*	≠	partir	*to leave*
monter	*to climb*	≠	descendre	*to go down*
		≠	tomber	*to fall*
naître	*to be born*	≠	mourir	*to die*

Verbs derived from the above verbs are also conjugated with **être**: **rentrer** *(to return)*, **revenir** *(to come back)*, and **devenir** *(to become)*, among others.

──────────── AGREEMENT OF THE PAST PARTICIPLE ────────────

The rules of agreement of the past participle depend on whether the auxiliary verb is **avoir** or **être**.

Être — When the auxiliary verb is **être**, the past participle agrees with the subject (review the section *What is a Subject?*, p. 24).

Pierre est **allé** au cinéma.
  | |
subject   past participle
     Lmasc. sing. (**allé**)⌋
Peter went to the movies.

Marie est **allée** au cinéma.
  | |
subject   past participle
    Lfem. sing. (**allé + e**)⌋
Mary went to the movies.

40

50

60

70

Paul et Marie sont **allés** au cinéma.
└──┬──┘   │
  subjects   past participle
      └masc. pl. (**allé** + **s**)┘
*Paul and Mary **went** to the movies.*

Avoir — When the auxiliary verb is **avoir**, the past participle agrees with the direct object, if the direct object comes before the verb in the sentence (review the section on direct objects, p. 104 and pronoun direct objects, p. 112). If there is no direct object or if the direct object comes after the verb, there is no agreement and the past participle remains in its masculine singular form.

Here are a few sentences where the past participle agrees with the direct object because the direct object precedes it.

Le **fauteuil** qu'il a **acheté** est confortable.
      └ masc. sing. ┘
*The **armchair** he **bought** is comfortable.*

La **chaise** qu'il a **achetée** est confortable.
      └ fem. sing. ┘
*The **chair** he **bought** is comfortable.*

Les **chaises** qu'il a **achetées** sont confortables.
      └ fem. pl. ┘
*The **chairs** he **bought** are comfortable.*

Le **fauteuil** et la **chaise** qu'il a **achetés** sont confortables.
      │   │   │
  masc. sing. + fem. sing.   masc. pl.
*The **armchair** and **the chair** he **bought** are comfortable.*

Remember the following when using the **passé composé:**
1. Determine whether the verb takes **avoir** or **être** as the auxiliary.
2. Depending on which auxiliary verb is required, apply the appropriate rules of agreement.

─────────────── **L'IMPARFAIT** (IMPERFECT) ───────────────

The **imparfait** is a simple tense formed by adding a set of endings to the stem of the verb. You will find those endings in your textbook.

Two English verb forms indicate that the **imparfait** should be used in French:

1. the verb form includes, or could include, *used to* → tells 120
   how things used to be

> *I **used to go** to France every year.*
> J'**allais** en France chaque année.
> |
>   imparfait

> *As a child I **went** to France every year.*
> |
>   could be replaced by *used to go* → imparfait
>   Comme enfant j'**allais** en France chaque année.

2. the verb form is in the past continuous tense → tells
   what was going on   130

> *At 10:00 P.M. last night I **was sleeping**.*
> A dix heures hier soir je **dormais**.
> |
>   imparfait

Except for these two English verb forms, the English verb
does not indicate whether you should use the **imparfait**
or the **passé composé**.

─────────── **SELECTION:** LE PASSÉ COMPOSÉ **OR** L'IMPARFAIT───────────

Whether to put a verb in the **passé composé** or the   140
imparfait often depends on the context. As a general
guideline, the difference in the two tenses is as follows:

> **le passé composé** → tells "what happened"
> **l'imparfait** → tells "how things used to be" or
>   "what was going on"

Here is an example. The same form of the verb *to go,*
namely "went," is used in the two answers below: "I *went*
to school." However, the tense of the French verb **aller** *(to
go)* changes depending on the question asked.

- "What happened?"   150

> QUESTION: *What **did** you **do** yesterday?*
> ANSWER: *I **went** to school.*
>   The question and answer tell "what happened yesterday;"
>   therefore, "did do" and "went" are in the **passé composé**.
> QUESTION: Qu'est-ce que tu **as fait** hier?
> ANSWER: Je **suis allée** à l'école.

- "How things used to be"

> QUESTION: *What **did** you **do** when you were a child?*
> ANSWER: *I **went** to school.*   160
>   The question and answer tell "how things used to be;"
>   therefore, "did go" and "went" are in the **imparfait**.

QUESTION: Qu'est-ce que tu **faisais** quand tu étais enfant?
ANSWER: J'**allais** à l'école.

As you can see from the two French examples above, the tense of the answer is usually the same as the tense of the question.

- "What was going on?"

Since the **imparfait** and the **passé composé** indicate actions that took place during the same time period in the past, the two tenses are often intermingled in a sentence or a story.

> *I **was reading** when he **arrived**.*
> Both actions "reading" and "arrived" took place at the same time. What was going on? I was reading → **imparfait**. What happened? He arrived → **passé composé**.
> Je **lisais** quand il **est arrivé**.
> imparfait   passé composé

Sometimes both tenses are possible, but usually one of the two is more logical. Consult your textbook.

— REVIEW —

Circle the verbs that would be put in the **imparfait** and underline the verbs that would be put in the **passé composé**.

Last summer, I *went* to France with my family. Everyone *was* very excited when we *arrived* at the airport. While my mother *checked* the luggage and my father *handled* the tickets, my little sister Mary *ran* away. My parents *dropped* everything and *tried* to catch her, but she *ducked* behind the counter. Finally, a manager *grabbed* her and *brought* her back to us. She *was crying* because she *was* sad she *was leaving* her dog for two weeks. Everyone *comforted* her and she *went* on the plane and *left* with a smile.

WHAT IS THE PLUPERFECT TENSE?

The **PLUPERFECT TENSE** is used to express an action
completed in the past before another action
or event which also occurred in the past.[1]

She suddenly *remembered* that she *had forgotten* her keys.
         simple past (past definite)   pluperfect
                  1   2

Both actions 1 and 2 occurred in the past, but action 2
preceded action 1. Therefore, action 2 is in the pluperfect.

IN ENGLISH

The pluperfect is formed with the auxiliary **had** + the past
participle of the main verb: *I had walked, he had seen,* etc.
In conversation *had* is often shortened to *'d.*

Don't forget that verb tenses indicate the time that an
action occurs. Therefore, when verbs in the same sentence
are in the same tense, the actions took place at the same
time. In order to show that actions took place at different
times, different tenses must be used.

Look at the following examples:

The mother *was crying* because her son *was leaving.*
        past continuous   past continuous
           1   1
Action 1 and action 2 took place at the same time.

The mother *was crying* because her son *had left.*
        past continuous   pluperfect
           1   2
Action 2 took place before action 1.

IN FRENCH

The pluperfect, **LE PLUS-QUE-PARFAIT** in French, is formed
with the auxiliary verb **avoir** or **être** in the **imparfait** +
the past participle of the main verb: **j'avais marché** *(I had
walked),* **elle était allée** *(she had gone).*

---

[1]You can compare this tense with the future perfect which is used when two actions
will happen at different times in the future and you want to stress which action will
precede the other (see *What is the Future Perfect Tense?*, p. 67).

The rules of agreement of the past participle are the same as for the **passé composé** (see p. 57).

A verb is put in the **plus-que-parfait** in order to stress that the action of that verb took place before the action of a verb in either the **passé composé** or the **imparfait**.

Observe the sequence of events expressed by the past tenses in the following time-line:

VERB TENSE:	Pluperfect	Simple past Past continuous	Present
	Plus-que-parfait	Passé composé Imparfait	Présent
	- 2	- 1	0

| | x | x | x |

TIME ACTION TAKES PLACE:	$0 \rightarrow$ now
	$-1 \rightarrow$ before 0
	$-2 \rightarrow$ before -1

- same verb tense → same moment in time

  *The mother **was crying** because her son **was leaving**.*
  La mère **pleurait** parce que son fils **partait**.
  imparfait   imparfait
  -1   -1

  Two actions in the **imparfait** (point -1) show that they took place at the same time in the past (before 0).

- different verb tenses → different times

  *The mother **was crying** because her son **had left**.*
  La mère **pleurait** parce que son fils **était parti**.
  imparfait   plus-que-parfait
  -1   -2

  The action in the **plus-que-parfait** (point -2) occurred before the action in the **imparfait** (point -1).

CAREFUL — You cannot always rely on spoken English to determine when to use the pluperfect in French. In many cases, English usage permits the use of the simple past to describe an action that preceded another, if it is clear which action came first.

*The teacher **wanted** to know if I **prepared** the lesson.*
simple past   simple past

*The teacher **wanted** to know if I **had prepared** the lesson.*
simple past   pluperfect

Although the two sentences above mean the same thing, only the sequence of tenses in the second sentence would be correct in French.

80

> Le professeur **voulait** savoir si j'**avais préparé** la leçon.
>
> imparfait   plus-que-parfait
>
> -1   -2

> Le professeur **a voulu** savoir si j'**avais préparé** la leçon.
>
> passé composé   plus-que-parfait
>
> -1   -2

> The action in the **plus-que-parfait** (point -2) stresses that it was completed before the other action (point -1) which could be in the **imparfait** or the **passé composé** depending on the context.

90

— REVIEW —

In the parentheses, number the verbs according to the time-line on p. 62.

- On the line below, indicate if the verb would be in the past (P) or pluperfect (PP) in French.

1. This morning Mary read the book she bought yesterday.

                 (-____)   (-____)

             _____   _____

2. After lunch, Paul asked who'd called him that morning.

                 (-____)   (-____)

             _____   _____

CHAPTER

20

WHAT IS THE FUTURE TENSE?

1 The FUTURE TENSE indicates that an action will take place some time in the future.

I'll see you tomorrow.

IN ENGLISH ——————————————

The future tense is formed with the auxiliary **will** or **shall** + the dictionary form of the main verb. In conversation, *shall* and *will* are often shortened to *'ll*.

Paul and Mary *will do* their homework tomorrow.
10 I*'ll leave* tonight.

IN FRENCH ——————————————

You do not need an auxiliary to show that an action will take place in the future. Future time is indicated by a simple tense.

Regular verbs use the infinitive as the stem for the future.

INFINITIVE	STEM	
aimer	aimer-	*to love*
finir	finir-	*to finish*
20	vendre	vendr-	*to sell*
	(the final "e" is dropped)	

Irregular verbs have irregular future stems which must be memorized.

INFINITIVE	STEM	
aller	ir-	*to go*
venir	viendr-	*to come*
avoir	aur-	*to have*
être	ser-	*to be*

30 Notice that whatever the stem, regular or irregular, the sound of the letter "r" is always heard before the future ending. Your textbook will give you the future endings to be added to the future stems to form the future tense.

CAREFUL — While English uses the present tense after expressions such as *as soon as, when,* and *by the time,* which introduce an action that will take place in the future, French uses the future tense.

> *As soon as he **returns**, I **shall call**.*
>   present   future
>
> Dès qu'il **reviendra**, je **téléphonerai**.
>   future   future
>
> "as soon as he *will come* . . ."

> *She **will come** when she **is** ready.*
>   future   present
>
> Elle **viendra** quand elle **sera** prête.
>   future   future
>   ". . . when she *will be* ready"

French is stricter than English in its use of tenses.

─────────── THE IMMEDIATE FUTURE ───────────

In English and in French an action which will occur some time in the future can also be expressed without using the future tense itself, but with a construction which implies the future. This construction is called the IMMEDIATE FUTURE.

IN ENGLISH

The immediate future is expressed with the verb *to go* in the present continuous tense + the infinitive of the main verb: *I am going to walk, she is going to see*, etc.

> similar meaning
>
> *I am going **to sing**.*   *I **shall sing**.*
> present continuous   future tense
> of *to go* + infinitive

IN FRENCH

The same construction exists in French. It is called "LE FUTUR IMMÉDIAT" or "LE FUTUR PROCHE" because the future action is considered nearer at hand than an action expressed by a verb in the future tense.

The immediate future is formed with the verb **aller** *(to go)* in the present tense + the infinitive of the main verb: **je vais marcher** *(I'm going to walk)*, **elle va voir** *(she's going to see)*.

Look at the difference between the forms of the immediate future and the future tense.

Je **vais chanter.**   Je **chanterai.**

present of **aller** + infinitive   future tense
immediate future

I am going to sing.   *I will sing.*

present of *to go* + infinitive   future tense
immediate future

In conversational French, the immediate future often replaces the future tense.

— *REVIEW* —

Indicate the tense as it is in the English sentence: present (P), or future (F).
▪ Indicate the tense of the verb as it would be in a French sentence.

1. As soon as we finish our meal, we'll leave.

    IN ENGLISH: _____   _____

    IN FRENCH: _____   _____

2. We will speak French when we go to France this summer.

    IN ENGLISH: _____   _____

    IN FRENCH: _____   _____

WHAT IS THE FUTURE PERFECT TENSE?

The **FUTURE PERFECT TENSE** is used to express an action which will occur before another action in the future or before a specific time in the future.[1]

By the time we leave, he *will have finished.*

future event
2

future perfect
1

Both actions 1 and 2 will occur at some future time, but action 1 will be completed before action 2 takes place. Therefore, action 1 is in the future perfect tense.

I won't meet him. I *shall have left* before he arrives.

future perfect
1

future event
2

Both action 1 and event 2 will occur at some future time, but action 1 will be completed before a specific event in the future. Therefore, action 1 is in the future perfect tense.

IN ENGLISH

The future perfect is formed with the auxiliary *will* (or *shall) have* + the past participle of the main verb: *I shall have walked, she will have gone.* In conversation *shall* and *will* are often shortened to *'ll.*

The future perfect is often used following expressions such as *by then, by that time, by* + a date.

By the end of the month, he *'ll have graduated.*
By June, I *'ll have saved* enough to buy a car.

IN FRENCH

The future perfect, **LE FUTUR ANTÉRIEUR** in French, is formed with the auxiliary **avoir** or **être** in the future tense + the past participle of the main verb: **j'aurai marché** *(I'll have walked),* **elle sera allée** *(she'll have gone).*

The rules of agreement of the past participle are the same as for the **passé composé** (see p. 57).

---

[1]You can compare this tense to the pluperfect which is used when two actions occurred at different times in the past and you want to stress which action preceded the other (see *What is the Pluperfect Tense?*, p. 61).

As in English, a verb is put in the **futur antérieur** tense in order to stress that the action of that verb will take place before the action of a verb in the future, or before a specific future time.

Observe the sequence of events expressed by the future tenses in the following time-line:

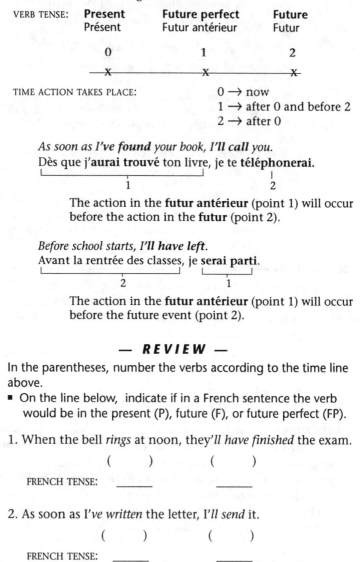

VERB TENSE: **Present**   **Future perfect**   **Future**
Présent   Futur antérieur   Futur

0   1   2

—x——————x————x—

TIME ACTION TAKES PLACE: 0 → now
1 → after 0 and before 2
2 → after 0

*As soon as I've **found** your book, I'll **call** you.*
Dès que j'**aurai trouvé** ton livre, je te **téléphonerai**.
        1   2

The action in the **futur antérieur** (point 1) will occur before the action in the **futur** (point 2).

*Before school starts, I'll **have left**.*
Avant la rentrée des classes, je **serai parti**.
        2   1

The action in the **futur antérieur** (point 1) will occur before the future event (point 2).

— *REVIEW* —

In the parentheses, number the verbs according to the time line above.

- On the line below, indicate if in a French sentence the verb would be in the present (P), future (F), or future perfect (FP).

1. When the bell *rings* at noon, they'*ll have finished* the exam.

            (   )   (   )

FRENCH TENSE: _____   _____

2. As soon as I'*ve written* the letter, I'*ll send* it.

            (   )   (   )

FRENCH TENSE: _____   _____

WHAT IS MEANT BY MOOD?

1

MOOD in the grammatical sense is a term
applied to verb tenses.

Different moods serve different purposes. For instance,
verb tenses which state a fact belong to one mood *(you are
studying, you studied)*, and the verb tense which gives
orders belongs to another *(Study!)*. Some moods have multiple tenses, others have only one tense.

You should recognize the names of moods so that you
will know what your French textbook is referring to when
it uses these terms. You will learn when to use the various 10
moods as you learn verbs and their tenses.

IN ENGLISH ─────────────────────────────────
Verbs can be in one of three moods:

1. The INDICATIVE MOOD is used to state the action of the
   verb; that is, to *indicate* facts. This is the most common
   mood, and most of the verb forms that you use in
   everyday conversation belong to the indicative mood.
   The majority of the tenses studied in this handbook
   belong to the indicative mood: for instance, the present 20
   tense (see p. 51), the past tense (see p. 56), and the
   future tense (p. 64).

   > Paul *studies* French.
   > present indicative

   > Mary *was* here.
   > past indicative

   > They *will come* tomorrow.
   > future indicative 30

2. The IMPERATIVE MOOD is used to give commands or
   orders (see *What is the Imperative?*, p. 71). This mood is
   not divided into tenses.

   > Paul, *study* French now!
   > Mary, *be* home on time!

3. The SUBJUNCTIVE MOOD is used to express an attitude or feeling toward the action of the verb; it is *subjective* about it (see *What is the Subjunctive?*, p. 78). In English, this mood is not divided into tenses.

> The school requires that students *study* French.
> I wish that Mary *were* here.
> The teacher recommends that he *do* his homework.

IN FRENCH

Verbs can be in one of four moods.

1. As in English, the INDICATIVE MOOD is the most common, and most of the tenses you will learn belong to this mood.

2. As in English, the IMPERATIVE MOOD is used to give orders and it is not divided into tenses.

3. Unlike English, the SUBJUNCTIVE MOOD is used very frequently. It has two main tenses: the present subjunctive and the perfect subjunctive.

   Textbooks use the term "present subjunctive" to distinguish it from the "present indicative" and the "present conditional."

4. French grammar also recognizes a mood called the CONDITIONAL MOOD which has two tenses: the present conditional and the past conditional (see *What is the Conditional?*, p. 73).

   Textbooks use the term "present conditional" to distinguish it from the "present indicative" and "present subjunctive."

When there is no reference to mood, the tense belongs to the most common mood, the indicative.

WHAT IS THE IMPERATIVE?

The **IMPERATIVE** is used to give someone an order.

The **AFFIRMATIVE IMPERATIVE** is an order to do something.

Come here!

The **NEGATIVE IMPERATIVE** is an order not to do something.

Don't come here!

IN ENGLISH

There are two types of command, depending on who is told to do, or not to do, something.

1. **"YOU" COMMAND** — When an order is given to one or more persons, the dictionary form of the verb is used.

AFFIRMATIVE IMPERATIVE	NEGATIVE IMPERATIVE
Answer the phone.	*Don't answer* the phone.
Clean your room.	*Don't clean* your room.
Speak softly.	*Don't speak* softly.

2. **"WE" COMMAND** — When an order is given to oneself as well as to others, the phrase "let's" (a contraction of *let us*) is used + the dictionary form of the verb.

AFFIRMATIVE IMPERATIVE	NEGATIVE IMPERATIVE
Let's leave.	*Let's not leave.*
Let's go to the movies.	*Let's not go* to the movies.

IN FRENCH

As in English, there are affirmative and negative commands. However, there are three forms because the "you" command has both a familiar and a formal form.

To form the imperative, most verbs use the present tense, dropping the subject pronoun. Your textbook will go over the verbs that have an irregular imperative.

1. **"TU" COMMAND** — When an order is given to a person to whom one says **tu**, the **tu**-form of the present tense is used.

AFFIRMATIVE IMPERATIVE	NEGATIVE IMPERATIVE
Viens.	Ne **viens** pas.
Come.	*Don't **come**.*
Prends le livre.	Ne **prends** pas le livre.
Take the book.	*Don't **take** the book.*

1
10
20
30

2. "VOUS" COMMAND — When an order is given to a person to whom one says **vous**, or to more than one person, the **vous**-form of the present tense is used.

AFFIRMATIVE IMPERATIVE	NEGATIVE IMPERATIVE
Venez.	**Ne venez pas.**
Come.	*Don't come.*
Prenez le livre.	**Ne prenez pas** le livre.
Take the book.	*Don't take the book.*

3. "NOUS" COMMAND — When an order is given to oneself as well as to others, the **nous**-form of the present tense is used.

AFFIRMATIVE IMPERATIVE	NEGATIVE IMPERATIVE
Allons.	**N'allons pas.**
Let's go.	*Let's not go.*
Prenons le livre.	**Ne prenons pas** le livre.
Let's take the book.	*Let's not take the book.*

In English and in French the absence of the subject pronoun in the sentence is a good indication that you are dealing with an imperative and not a present tense (see *What is the Present Tense?*, p. 51).

Vous répondez au téléphone .
You answer the phone.
   |
   present

Répondez au téléphone.
Answer the phone.
   |
imperative

— *R E V I E W* —

I. Change the sentences below to the imperative affirmative.

1. You should study every evening.

_____

2. We go to the movies once a week.

_____

II. Change the following sentences to the imperative negative.

1. You shouldn't sleep in class.

_____

2. We don't speak in class.

_____

WHAT IS THE CONDITIONAL?

The **CONDITIONAL** forms of a verb get their name because they
are primarily used in sentences which imply a condition.

1

If I were offered the job, I *would take* it.
　　　condition　　　　　　conditional

The conditional has a present and past tense.

————————— PRESENT CONDITIONAL —————————

IN ENGLISH

The present conditional is made up of two words: the
auxiliary ***would*** + the dictionary form of the main verb:
I would eat.

10

The present conditional is used in the following ways:

1. as a polite form with *like* and in polite requests

> I *would like* to eat.
> More polite than "I want to eat."

> *Would* you please close the door.
> "Please close the door" is softened by the use of *would*.

2. in the result clause of a hypothetical statement

20

A **HYPOTHETICAL STATEMENT** includes a condition that does
not exist at the present time, but could possibly
become a reality one day.

　　　condition　　　　result clause
If Paul had money, he *would buy* a car.
　subject　verb　　subject　verb in the conditional

The statement above is hypothetical because Paul
does not have money at the present time; but there is
the possibility that he will have money some day and,
therefore, be able to buy a car.

30

A **CLAUSE** is a part of a sentence composed of a group of
words containing a subject and a verb. In a hypothetical statement there are two types of clauses: the *if*-
clause and the result clause.

■ **IF-CLAUSE** — expresses the condition which must be
met. In the above example: "If Paul had money...."

- **RESULT CLAUSE** — expresses the result if the condition is met. In the above example: "he would buy a car."

3. in an indirect statement to express a future-in-the-past

An **INDIRECT STATEMENT** repeats, or reports, but does not quote, someone's words, as opposed to a **DIRECT STATEMENT** which is a word-for-word quotation of what someone said. In written form a direct statement is always between quotation marks.

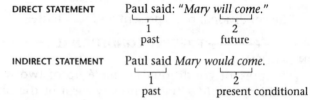

DIRECT STATEMENT   Paul said: "*Mary will come.*"
                                    1   2
                                   past   future

INDIRECT STATEMENT   Paul said *Mary would come.*
                                    1   2
                                   past   present conditional

In an indirect statement, action 2 *(Mary would come)* is called a **FUTURE-IN-THE-PAST** because it takes place after another action in the past *(Paul said)*. In the direct statement, action 2 is merely a quotation in the future tense.

IN FRENCH

Unlike English, you do not need an auxiliary to indicate the present conditional, **LE CONDITIONNEL PRÉSENT** in French. It is a simple tense formed with the future stem (see p. 64) + the imperfect endings: je parler**ais** (*I would speak*), il finir**ait** (*he would finish*), nous vendr**ions** (*we would sell*).

The present conditional is used in the same ways as in English:

1. as a polite form or in polite requests

Je **voudrais** un sandwich.
                 |
present conditional
I would like a sandwich.

Pourriez-vous fermer la porte?
                 |
present conditional
***Would** you please close the door?*

2. in the main clause of a hypothetical statement

Si Paul avait de l'argent, il **achèterait** une voiture.
                                      |
                              present conditional
*If Paul had money, he **would buy** a car.*

3. in an indirect statement to express a future-in-the-past

> Il a dit qu'il **viendrait**.
> present conditional
> *He said (that) he **would come**.*

> Je savais qu'il **pleuvrait**.
> present conditional
> *I knew (that) it **would rain**.*

CAREFUL — The auxiliary *would* does not correspond to the French conditional when it stands for *used to*, as in "she *would talk* while he painted." In this sentence, it means *used to talk* and requires the imperfect (see p. 59).

PAST CONDITIONAL

IN ENGLISH

The past conditional is made up of the auxiliary **would have** + the dictionary form of the main verb: *I would have eaten, he would have come.*

The past conditional is only used in the result clause of contrary-to-fact statements.

A statement is **CONTRARY-TO-FACT** when a condition was not met in the past and therefore the result was not realized.

> *if*-clause   result clause
> If I had had money, I *would have bought* a car.

The statement above is contrary-to-fact because the the person speaking didn't have money in the past and therefore did not buy a car.

> He *would have spoken* if he had known the truth.
> Contrary-to-fact: He did not speak
> because he didn't know the truth.

> If you had called us, we *would have come*.
> Contrary-to-fact: We did not come
> because you didn't call us.

IN FRENCH

The past conditional, **LE CONDITIONNEL PASSÉ** in French, is formed with the auxiliary **avoir** or **être** in the present conditional + the past participle of the main verb: **j'aurais mangé, elle serait allée** *(I would have eaten, she would have gone).* The same rules of agreement apply as for the **passé composé**, see p. 57.

As in English, the past conditional is used in the result clause of contrary-to-fact statements.

Il **aurait parlé**, s'il avait su la vérité.
*He **would have spoken**, if he had known the truth.*

——————————— SEQUENCE OF TENSES ———————————

Let us look at examples of hypothetical and contrary-to-fact statements so that you learn to use the appropriate tense in each clause.

Hypothetical and contrary-to-fact statements are easy to recognize because they are always made up of two clauses:

- the **IF-CLAUSE** (the clause that starts with *if,* **si** in French)
- the **RESULT CLAUSE**

In English and in French the *if*-clause can come before or after the result clause.

If he had come, I would have been happy.
I would have been happy *if he had come.*

The sequence of tenses is the same in English and in French. In both languages, the tense of one clause requires a certain tense in the other.

"IF"-CLAUSE → PRESENT PRÉSENT	RESULT CLAUSE → FUTURE FUTUR

If he comes, I shall be happy.
present   future

S'il **vient**, je **serai** contente.
présent   futur

"IF"-CLAUSE → SIMPLE PAST (PAST DEFINITE) IMPARFAIT	RESULT CLAUSE → PRESENT CONDITIONAL CONDITIONNEL PRÉSENT

If he came, I would be happy.
simple past   present conditional

S'il **venait**, je **serais** contente.
imparfait   conditionnel présent

130

140

150

160

160

"IF"-CLAUSE → PLUPERFECT	RESULT CLAUSE → PAST CONDITIONAL
PLUS-QUE-PARFAIT	**CONDITIONNEL PASSÉ**

*If he **had come**, I **would have been** happy.*
    pluperfect   past conditional

S'il **était venu**, j'**aurais été** contente.
    plus-que-parfait conditionnel passé

CAREFUL — Remember the tense of a clause remains the same no matter which clause comes first (see example above and below).

170

*I **would have been** happy if he **had come**.*
    past conditional   pluperfect

J'**aurais été** contente s'il **était venu**.
    conditionnel passé   plus-que-parfait

— REVIEW —

Write the tense you would use in French for each of the italicized verbs below: présent (P), futur (F) conditionnel présent (C), conditionnel passé (PC), imparfait (I), plus-que-parfait (PP).

1. Students *would do* their homework if they *had* time.

   _____   _____

2. If they *had had* an exam, they *would have studied*.

   _____   _____

3. When they *were* separated, he *would call* her every evening.

   _____   _____

4. We'll *be going* abroad, if we *have* the money.

   _____   _____

CHAPTER

25

WHAT IS THE SUBJUNCTIVE?

The **SUBJUNCTIVE** is a mood used to express a wish, hope, uncertainty or other similar attitude toward a fact or an idea. Since it stresses the subject's feelings about the fact or idea, it is usually *subjective* about them.

I wish he *were* here.
     | |
subject's subjunctive
wish

The teacher insisted that the homework *be* neat.
        | |
     subject's   subjunctive
     feelings

IN ENGLISH

The subjunctive verb form is difficult to recognize because it is spelled like other tenses of the verb: the dictionary form and the simple past (past definite) tense.

INDICATIVE	SUBJUNCTIVE
He *reads* a lot.	The course requires that he *read* a lot.
indicative present *to read*	subjunctive (same as dictionary form)
I *am* in Paris.	I wish I *were* in Paris.
indicative present *to be*	subjunctive (same as past tense)

The subjunctive is used in very few constructions. Besides the few examples above, it is used primarily in expressions such as: Long *live* the Republic! God *save* the Queen!

IN FRENCH

The subjunctive is used very frequently; unfortunately English usage will rarely help you decide when to use it in French.

Here are a few suggestions as to how to approach the subjunctive when it is introduced in your French textbook.

1. When you learn the conjugation of verbs in the present tense of the subjunctive, it is useful to compare those forms to the present indicative. This will help you to remember what distinguishes one from the other.

2. Learn the verbs and expressions that require that the verb which follows be put in the subjunctive. Be careful, it is not the verb or the expression itself which is put in the subjunctive, it is the verb that follows. 40

Here are examples of verbs and expressions that trigger the use of the subjunctive in the following verb.

- a verb of desire: **vouloir** *(to want)*

  Je veux que tu **sois** sage.
  | |
  vouloir   **être**
  indicative   subjunctive
  *I want you **to be** good.*
  (word-for-word: "I want that you *be* good") 50

- an expression: **il faut que** *(it is necessary that)*

  Il faut que Paul **sache** parler français.
  | |
  falloir   **savoir**
  indicative   subjunctive
  *Paul must **know how** to speak French.*
  (word-for-word: "it is necessary that Paul *know how* to speak French")

- an adjective expressing an emotion: **être heureux** *(to be happy)* 60

  Je suis heureux que vous **veniez** ce soir.
  | |
  être   **venir**
  indicative   subjunctive
  *I am happy that you **are coming** this evening.*

Since the use of the subjunctive in English is so limited and not relevant to its use in French, we refer you to your textbook for an explanation of when this mood is appropriate in French.

WHAT IS AN ADJECTIVE?

¹ An **ADJECTIVE** is a word that describes a noun or a pronoun.
There are different types of adjectives which
are classified according to the way
they describe a noun or pronoun.

DESCRIPTIVE ADJECTIVE — A descriptive adjective indicates a quality, it tells what kind of noun it is (see p. 81).

> She read an *interesting* book.
> He has *brown* eyes.

¹⁰ **POSSESSIVE ADJECTIVE**— A possessive adjective shows possession, it tells whose noun it is (see p. 88).

> *His* book is lost.
> *Our* parents are away.

INTERROGATIVE ADJECTIVE — An interrogative adjective asks a question about a noun (see p. 93).

> *What* book is lost?
> *Which* parents did you speak to?

²⁰ **DEMONSTRATIVE ADJECTIVE** — A demonstrative adjective points out a noun (see p. 95).

> *This* teacher is excellent.
> *That* question is very appropriate.

IN ENGLISH ─────────────────────────
English adjectives usually do not change their form, regardless of the noun or pronouns described.

IN FRENCH ─────────────────────────
The principal difference between English and French adjectives is that while in English adjectives do not ³⁰ change their form, in French adjectives change in order to agree in gender and number with the noun or pronoun they modify.

WHAT IS A DESCRIPTIVE ADJECTIVE?

A **DESCRIPTIVE ADJECTIVE** is a word that indicates a quality of a   1
noun or pronoun. As the name implies, it
describes the noun or pronoun.

> The book is *interesting*.
> | |
>   noun   descriptive
>   described   adjective

IN ENGLISH────────────────────────────

A descriptive adjective does not change form, regardless of
the noun or pronoun it modifies.   10

> The students are *intelligent*.
> She is an *intelligent* person.
>> The adjective *intelligent* is the same although the persons
>> described are different in number *(students* is plural and
>> *person* is singular).

Descriptive adjectives are divided into two groups depending on how they are connected to the noun they modify.

1. A **PREDICATE ADJECTIVE** is connected to the noun it
   describes, always the subject of the sentence, by **LINKING**   20
   VERBS such as *to be, to feel, to look*.

> The children are *good*.
> | | |
>   noun   linking predicate
>   described verb   adjective

> The house looks *small*.
> | | |
>   noun   linking predicate
> described verb   adjective

2. An **ATTRIBUTIVE ADJECTIVE** is connected directly to the
   noun it describes and always precedes it.   30

> The *good* children were praised.
> | |
> attributive noun
>   adjective described

> The family lives in a *small* house.
> | |
>   attributive noun
>   adjective described

IN FRENCH ————————————————————————————

As in English, descriptive adjectives can be identified as predicate or attributive adjectives according to the way they are connected to the noun they describe.

French descriptive adjectives differ in two important ways from English descriptive adjectives.

1. While English descriptive adjectives never change form, all French descriptive adjectives, predicate and attributive, change form in order to agree in gender and number with the noun or pronoun they modify.

   Most adjectives add an "-e" to the masculine form to make the feminine form and an "-s" to the masculine singular or the feminine singular form to make it plural.

*the **blue** book*	le livre **bleu** | | masc. masc. sing. sing.
*the **blue** dress*	la robe **bleue** | | fem. fem. (**bleu** + e) sing. sing.
*the **blue** books*	les livres **bleus** | | masc. masc. (**bleu** + s) pl. pl.
*the **blue** dresses*	les robes **bleues** | | fem. fem. (**bleu** + es) pl. pl.

2. While English attributive descriptive adjectives always come before the noun they modify, most, but not all, French attributive descriptive adjectives come after the noun they modify.

   Elle lit un **livre intéressant**.
   *She is reading an **interesting book**.*

   However, some common French descriptive adjectives come before the noun they modify.

   Paul est un **beau garçon** et Marie est une **jolie fille**.
   *Paul is a **handsome boy** and Mary is a **pretty girl**.*

   Your textbook will tell you, and you will have to learn, which French descriptive adjectives precede and which follow the noun they modify.

---------------------- **NOUNS USED AS ADJECTIVES** ----------------------

Occasionally, a noun is used as an adjective; that is, it is used to modify another noun.

IN ENGLISH

When a noun is used to describe another noun, the structure is as follows: the describing noun (adjective) + the noun described.

French is difficult.   The *French* class is interesting.
    | | |
  noun   adjective   noun described

Chemistry is difficult.   The *chemistry* books are expensive.
    | | |
  noun   adjective   noun described

IN FRENCH

It is important that you recognize a noun acting as an adjective because it remains a noun and does not change form. In the examples below, you will see that the noun described and the noun acting as an adjective have different genders and numbers.

When a noun is used as an adjective, the structure is as follows: the noun described + **de** *(of)* + the describing noun (adjective) without an article.

the French class   la **classe** de **français**
  | | | |
le **français**   la **classe**   fem. sing.   masc. sing.
                                  noun   noun/
                                  described   adjective

the chemistry books   les **livres** de **chimie**
     | | | |
la **chimie**   les **livres**   masc. pl.   fem. sing.
                                  noun   noun/
                                  described   adjective

— *R E V I E W* —

Circle the adjectives in the sentences below.
- Draw an arrow from the adjective you circled to the noun or pronoun described.

1. The young man was reading a French newspaper.

2. She looked pretty in her new red dress.

3. It is interesting.

4. The old piano could still produce good music.

5. Paul was tired after his long walk.

CHAPTER

28

WHAT IS MEANT BY COMPARISON OF ADJECTIVES?

The term **COMPARISON OF ADJECTIVES** is used when two or more persons or things have the same quality indicated by a descriptive adjective and we want to show which of these persons or things has a greater, lesser, or equal degree of that quality.

comparison of adjectives
| |
Paul is *tall* but Mary is *taller*.
| |
adjective   adjective
modifies *Paul*   modifies *Mary*

Both nouns, Paul and Mary, have the same quality indicated by the adjective *tall,* and we want to show that Mary has a greater degree of that quality (i.e., she is *taller* than Paul).

In English and in French there are two types of comparison: comparative and superlative.

─────────────── **COMPARATIVE** ───────────────

The comparative compares a quality of a person or thing with the same quality in another person or thing. The comparison can indicate that one or the other has more, less, or the same amount of that quality.

IN ENGLISH

Let's go over the three degrees of comparison:

1. The comparison of **GREATER DEGREE** (more) is formed differently depending on the length of the adjective being compared:

- short adjective + *-er* + *than*

  Paul is tall*er than* Mary.
  She is pretti*er than* her sister.

- *more* + longer adjective + *than*

  Paul is *more* intelligent *than* Mary.
  His car is *more* expensive *than* ours.

2. The comparison of **LESSER DEGREE** (less) is formed as follows: *not as* + adjective *as*, or *less* + adjective + *than*.

Mary is *not as* tall *as* Paul.
My car is *less* expensive *than* your car.

3. The comparison of EQUAL DEGREE (same) is formed as follows: *as* + adjective + *as*.

> Paul is *as* tall *as* Mary.
> My car is *as* expensive *as* yours.

IN FRENCH

There are the same three degrees of comparison of adjectives as in English.

Like all French adjectives, French comparative adjectives
agree with the noun they modify. In the case of comparative adjectives which describe more than one noun, they
agree in gender and number with the subject.

1. The comparison of GREATER DEGREE is formed as follows:
   plus *(more)* + adjective + **que** *(than)*.

> Paul est **plus** actif **que** Marie.
> agrees with subject → Paul
> *Paul is **more** active **than** Mary.*

2. The comparison of LESSER DEGREE is formed as follows:
   moins *(less)* + adjective + **que** *(than)*.

> Marie est **moins** active **que** Paul.
> agrees with subject → Marie
> *Mary is **less** active **than** Paul.*

3. The comparison of EQUAL DEGREE is formed as follows:
   aussi *(as)* + adjective + **que** *(as)*.

> Marie est **aussi** active **que** Paul.
> *Mary is **as** active **as** Paul.*

───────────────── **SUPERLATIVE** ─────────────────

The superlative is used to stress the highest and lowest
degrees of a quality.

IN ENGLISH

Let's go over the two degrees of the superlative:

1. The superlative of GREATEST DEGREE is formed differently
   depending on the length of the adjective.

   ▪ *the* + short adjective + *-est*

> Mary is *the* smart*est*.
> My car is *the* cheap*est* on the market.

■ *the most* + long adjective

80

Mary is *the most* intelligent.
His car is *the most* expensive.

2. The superlative of LOWEST DEGREE is formed as follows: *the least* + adjective.

Paul is *the least* active.
His car is *the least* expensive.

IN FRENCH

There are the same two degrees of the superlative:

90

1. The superlative of GREATEST DEGREE is formed as follows: **le, la,** or **les** (depending on the gender and number of the noun described) + **plus** *(most)* + adjective.

Marie est **la plus** active de la famille.
　　　　　fem. sing.
*Mary is **the most** active in the family.*

Paul est **le plus** grand.
　　　　masc. sing.
*Paul is **the tallest**.*

100

Marie et Paul sont **les plus** intelligents de la classe.
　　　　　　　　masc. pl.
*Mary and Paul are **the most** intelligent in the class.*

2. The superlative of LOWEST DEGREE is formed as follows: **le, la,** or **les** (depending on the gender and number of the noun described) + **moins** *(less)* + adjective.

Paul est **le moins** actif de la classe.
　　　　　masc. sing.
*Paul is **the least** active in the classe.*

110

CAREFUL — In English and in French, a few adjectives have irregular forms of comparison which you will have to memorize individually.

ADJECTIVE	Cette pomme est **bonne**. *This apple is **good**.*
COMPARATIVE	Cette pomme est **meilleure**. *This apple is **better**.*
SUPERLATIVE	Cette pomme est **la meilleure**. *This apple is **the best**.*

— *REVIEW* —

I. Underline the superlative and comparative adjectives in the sentences below.

- Draw an arrow from the adjective to the noun it modifies.
- Circle the various degrees of comparison: superlative (S), comparative of greater degree (C+), comparative of equal degree (C=), or comparative of lesser degree (C-).

1. The teacher is older than the students.   S   C+   C=   C-

2. He is less intelligent than I am.   S   C+   C=   C-

3. Mary is as tall as Paul.   S   C+   C=   C-

4. That boy is the worst in the school.   (S)   C+   C=   C-

5. Paul is a better student than Mary.   S   C+   C=   C-

CHAPTER

29

WHAT IS A POSSESSIVE ADJECTIVE?

A **POSSESSIVE ADJECTIVE** is a word which describes a noun
by showing who possesses that noun.

> Whose house is that? It's *my* house.
>> *My* shows who possesses the noun *house*. The
>> possessor is "me." The object possessed is *house*.

IN ENGLISH

Like subject pronouns, possessive adjectives are identified
according to the person they represent (see p. 28).

SINGULAR POSSESSOR
1ST PERSON		my
2ND PERSON		your
3RD PERSON	MASCULINE	his
	FEMININE	her
	NEUTER	its

PLURAL POSSESSOR
1ST PERSON	our
2ND PERSON	your
3RD PERSON	their

A possessive adjective changes according to the possessor, regardless of the objects possessed.

> Is that John's house? Yes, it is *his* house.
> Is that Mary's house? Yes, it is *her* house.
>> Although the object possessed is the same *(house)*, different
>> possessive adjectives *(his* and *her)* are used because the pos-
>> sessors are different *(John* and *Mary).*

> Is that John's house? Yes, it is *his* house.
> Are those John's keys? Yes, they are *his* keys.
>> Although the objects possessed are different *(house* and
>> *keys)*, the same possessive adjective *(his)* is used because the
>> possessor is the same *(John).*

IN FRENCH

Like English, a French possessive adjective changes
according to the possessor, but unlike English it also
agrees, like all French adjectives, in gender and number
with the noun possessed.

For example, in the phrase **mon frère** *(my brother)* the 1ˢᵗ person singular possessor *(my)* is indicated by the first letter of the possessive adjective, **m-**, and the gender and number of the noun possessed, **frère** *(brother)*, which is masculine singular, is reflected in the masculine singular ending **-on**.

Let us see what happens when we change *my brother* to *my sister.*

> *I love **my** sister*
> J'aime **ma** sœur.
> | fem.sing. ending
>   1ˢᵗ pers. sing. possessor

> The first letter **m-** remains the same because the possessor is still the 1ˢᵗ person, but the ending changes to **-a** to agree with **sœur** which is feminine singular.

The pattern of possessive adjectives for a singular possessor is different from the pattern of possessive adjectives for a plural possessor. We have the divided the French possessive adjectives into these two groups.

─────────────── Sɪɴɢᴜʟᴀʀ ᴘᴏssᴇssᴏʀ ───────────────
my, your (tu-form), his, her, its

In French, each of these possessive adjectives has three forms depending on the gender and number of the noun possessed: the masculine singular, the feminine singular, and the plural (the same for both genders).

To choose the correct possessive adjective:

1. Indicate the possessor with the first letter of the possessive adjective.

my	**m-**
your	**t-** (**tu**-form)
his	
her	**s-**
its	

2. Choose the ending according to the gender and number of the noun possessed.

   - noun possessed is masculine singular (or feminine singular beginning with a vowel) → add **-on**

> Anne lit **mon** livre.   *Anne reads **my** book.*
> | masc. sing. | noun possessed
> Anne lit **ton** livre.   *Anne reads **your** book.*
> Anne lit **son** livre.   *Anne reads **her** (**his**) book.*

40 50 60 70 80

Paul connaît **mon** amie.   *Paul knows **my** friend.*
            | |
       fem. sing.   noun possessed
    begins with vowel
Paul connaît **ton** amie.   *Paul knows **your** friend.*
Paul connaît **son** amie.   *Paul knows **his (her)** friend.*

- noun possessed is feminine singular beginning with a consonant → add -a

Paul lit **ma** lettre.   *Paul reads **my** letter.*
          | |
     fem. sing.   noun possessed
Paul lit **ta** lettre.   *Paul reads **your** letter.*
Paul lit **sa** lettre.   *Paul reads **his (her)** letter.*

- noun possessed is plural → add -es

Anne lit **mes** livres.   *Anne reads **my** books.*
            | |
        masc. pl.   noun possessed

Paul lit **tes** lettres.   *Paul reads **your** letters.*
           |
        fem. pl.

Elle lit **ses** livres.   *She is reading **her (his)** books.*
           |
        masc. pl.

3. Select the proper form according to the two steps above.

Let us apply the above steps to examples:

*Paul is looking at **his** mother.*
   1. Possessor: *his* → 3rd pers. sing. → **s-**
   2. Noun possessed: **Mère** *(mother)* is feminine singular.
   3. Selection: **s-** + **-a**
Paul regarde **sa** mère.

*Paul is looking at **his** father.*
   1. Possessor: *his* → 3rd pers. sing. → **s-**
   2. Noun possessed: **Père** *(father)* is masculine singular.
   3. Selection: **s-** + **-on**
Paul regarde **son** père.

CAREFUL — Make sure that the ending of the possessive adjective agrees with the noun it modifies and not with the possessor.

──────────────── **PLURAL POSSESSOR** ────────────────
our, your (vous-form), **their**

In French, each of these possessive adjectives has only two forms depending on the number of the noun possessed; that is, whether the noun possessed in singular or plural.

- noun possessed is singular → **notre, votre,** or **leur**

Marie est **notre** fille.	*Mary is **our** daughter.*
	noun possessed singular
Paul lit **votre** lettre.	*Paul reads **your** letter.*
Ils lisent **leur** lettre	*They read **their** letter.*

- noun possessed is plural → **nos, vos,** or **leurs** 130

Les parents sont **nos** amis.	*The parents are **our** friends.*
	noun possessed plural
Anne lit **vos** livres.	*Anne reads **your** books.*
Elles lisent **leurs** lettres.	*They read **their** letters.*

Although **votre,** and **vos** are classified as "the second person plural," they can refer to just one person when used as a formal form of address (see p. 29).

CAREFUL — Make sure that you use the same "you" form, either familiar or formal, for the verb and the possessive 140 adjective: *"You* are reading *your* letter" would be either "**Tu** lis **ta** lettre" or "**Vous** lisez **votre** lettre."

─────────── **SUMMARY** ───────────

Here is a chart you can use as a reference.

POSSESSOR SINGULAR		NOUN POSSESSED	
		SINGULAR	PLURAL
	MASC.	mon	
my	FEM. + VOWEL	mon	mes
	FEM.	ma	
your	MASC.	ton	
(tu form)	FEM. + VOWEL	ton	tes
	FEM.	ta	
	MASC.	son	
his, her, its	FEM. + VOWEL	son	ses
	FEM.	sa	
POSSESSOR PLURAL		NOUN POSSESSED	
		SINGULAR	PLURAL
our		notre	nos
your (vous form)		votre	vos
their		leur	leurs

150
160

— REVIEW —

Circle the possessive adjectives in the sentences below.
- Draw an arrow from the possessive adjective to the noun it modifies.
- Circle singular (S) or plural (P) to indicate the ending of the French possessive adjective.
- Using the charts in this section, fill in the French possessive adjective in the French sentences below.

1. I took my books home.

    POSSESSIVE ADJECTIVE IN FRENCH: masculine   S   P

    J'ai pris _____ livres à la maison.

2. Mary borrowed your [familiar] car.

    POSSESSIVE ADJECTIVE IN FRENCH: feminine   S   P

    Marie a emprunté _____ voiture.

3. Paul looks like our mother.

    POSSESSIVE ADJECTIVE IN FRENCH: feminine   S   P

    Paul ressemble à _____ mère.

4. Your [plural] clothes are expensive.

    POSSESSIVE ADJECTIVE IN FRENCH: masculine   S   P

    _____ vêtements sont chers.

WHAT IS AN INTERROGATIVE ADJECTIVE?

An **INTERROGATIVE ADJECTIVE** is a word that asks for information about a noun.

> *Which* book do you want?
>
> asks information about the noun *book*

IN ENGLISH

The words **which** and **what** are interrogative adjectives when they come in front of a noun and are used to ask a question about that noun.

> *Which* teacher is teaching the course?
> *What* courses are you taking?

IN FRENCH

There is only one interrogative adjective, **quel**. It changes to agree in gender and number with the noun it modifies. Therefore, in order to say *"which* book" or *"what* dress," start by analyzing the noun *book* or *dress.*

- noun modified is masculine singular → **quel**
  > **Quel** livre est sur la table?
  > **Livre** *(book)* is masculine singular,
  > so the word for "which" must be masculine singular.
  > **What** *book is on the table?*

- noun modified is masculine plural → **quels**
  > **Quels** livres sont sur la table?
  > **Livres** *(books)* is masculine plural,
  > so the word for "what" must be masculine plural.
  > **What** *books are on the table?*

- noun modified is feminine singular → **quelle**
  > **Quelle** robe voulez-vous?
  > **Robe** *(dress)* is feminine singular,
  > so the word for "what" must be feminine singular.
  > **Which** *dress do you want?*

- noun modified is feminine plural → **quelles**
  > **Quelles** robes voulez-vous?
  > **Robes** *(dresses)* is feminine plural,
  > so the word for "what" must be feminine plural.
  > **Which** *dresses do you want?*

1

10

20

30

In the sentences above, the noun which the interrogative adjective modifies is easy to identify because the noun and the adjective are next to one another. However, the noun modified is harder to identify when it is separated from the interrogative adjective. As you can see in the examples below, restructuring the sentences will help you identify the noun with which the interrogative adjective must agree.

> **What** is your address?
> Restructure: "What address is yours?"
> **Quelle** est votre adresse?
> |_____|
>   fem. sing.

> **Which** are his favorite books?
> Restructure: "Which books are his favorite?"
> **Quels** sont ses livres préférés?
> |_____|
>   masc. pl.

CAREFUL — The word *what* is not always an interrogative adjective. In the sentence *"What is on the table?"* it is an interrogative pronoun (see *What is an Interrogative Pronoun?*, p. 133). It is important that you distinguish one from the other because, in French, different words are used and they follow different rules.

— REVIEW —

Circle the interrogative adjectives in the sentences below.
- Draw an arrow from the interrogative adjective to the noun it modifies.
- Indicate if the noun modified is singular (S) or plural (P).
- Fill in the French interrogative adjective in the French sentences below.

1. Which courses are you taking?

   NOUN MODIFIED IN FRENCH: masculine   S   P

   _____ cours suivez-vous?

2. What is your favorite city?

   NOUN MODIFIED IN FRENCH: feminine   S   P

   _____ est ta ville préférée?

WHAT IS A DEMONSTRATIVE ADJECTIVE?

A **DEMONSTRATIVE ADJECTIVE** is a word used
to point out a noun.

This book is interesting.
│
points out the noun *book*

IN ENGLISH

The demonstrative adjectives are **this** and **that** in the singular and **these** and **those** in the plural. They are rare
examples of English adjectives agreeing in number with
the noun they modify: *this* changes to *these* and *that*
changes to *those* when they modify a plural noun.

SINGULAR	PLURAL
this cat	*these* cats
that man	*those* men

This and *these* refer to a person or object near the speaker, and *that* and *those* refer to a person or object away from
the speaker.

IN FRENCH

There is only one demonstrative adjective, **ce**. It changes
to agree in gender and number with the noun it modifies.
Therefore, in order to say *"that* book" or *"this* dress," start
by analyzing the noun *book* or *dress*.

- noun modified is masculine singular and starts with a
  consonant → **ce**

    Ce livre est sur la table.
    Livre *(book)* is masculine singular,
    so the word for "this" must be masculine singular.
    This (or that) book is on the table.

- noun modified is masculine singular and starts with a
  vowel → **cet**

    Cet appartement est grand.
    Appartement *(apartment)* is masculine singular.
    Since it begins with a vowel, the word for "this" must be **cet**.
    This (or that) apartment is large.

- noun modified is feminine singular → **cette**

  Cette robe est jolie.

  > **Robe** *(dress)* is feminine singular,
  > so the word for "this" must be feminine singular.

  *This (or **that**) dress is pretty.*

- noun modified is plural → **ces**

  Ces livres sont sur la table.

  > **Livres** *(books)* is plural,
  > so the word for "these" must be plural.

  *These (or **those**) books are on the table.*

To distinguish between what is close to the speaker *(this, these)* from what is far from the speaker *(that, those)* **-ci** or **-là** can be added after the noun: **-ci** indicates that the noun is close to the speaker, **-là** that the noun is far from the speaker.

> **Ces** livres-**ci** sont chers; **ces** livres-**là** ne sont pas chers.
> *These books **(here)** are expensive; those books **(there)** are not expensive.*

— REVIEW —

Circle the demonstrative adjectives in the sentences below.
- Draw an arrow from the demonstrative adjective to the noun it modifies.
- Circle if the noun modified is singular (S) or plural (P).
- Fill in the French demonstrative adjective in the French sentences below.

1. They prefer that restaurant.

   Noun modified in French: masculine   S   P

   Ils préfèrent _____ restaurant.

2. This test is too hard.

   Noun modified in French: masculine   S   P

   _____ examen est trop difficile.

3. These houses are expensive.

   Noun modified in French: feminine   S   P

   _____ maisons sont chères.

WHAT IS AN ADVERB?

An **ADVERB** is a word that describes a verb, an adjective,
   or another adverb. It indicates manner,
   degree, time, place.[1]

Mary drives *well*.
| |
verb adverb

The house is *very* big.
| |
adverb adjective

The girl ran *too quickly*.
| |
adverb adverb

IN ENGLISH ───────────────────────────────

There are different types of adverbs:

- an **ADVERB OF MANNER** answers the question *how?* Adverbs
  of manner are the most common and they are easy to
  recognize because they end with *-ly*.

  Mary sings *beautifully*.
  Beautifully describes the verb *sings*; it tells you how Mary sings.

- an **ADVERB OF DEGREE** answers the question *how much?*
  Paul does *well* in class.

- an **ADVERB OF TIME** answers the question *when?*
  He will come *soon*.

- an **ADVERB OF PLACE** answers the question *where?*
  The old were left *behind*.

IN FRENCH ───────────────────────────────

Most adverbs of manner can be recognized by the ending
-**ment** which corresponds to the English ending *-ly*.

joli**ment**	*beautifully*
générale**ment**	*generally*
heureuse**ment**	*happily*

---

[1]In English and in French, the structure for comparing adverbs is the same as the structure for comparing adjectives (see *What is Meant by Comparison of Adjectives?*,
p. 84).

You will have to memorize adverbs as vocabulary items. The most important fact for you to remember is that adverbs are invariable; ie., they never change form.

40

———————— Adverb or adjective? ————————

Because adverbs are invariable and French adjectives must agree with the noun they modify, it is important that you distinguish one from the other. When you write a sentence in French, always make sure that adjectives agree with the noun or pronoun they modify and that adverbs remain unchanged.

>   The **tall** girl talked **rapidly**.
>
>   *Tall* modifies the noun *girl;* it is an adjective. *Rapidly* modifies the verb *talked* (it describes how the girl talked); it is an adverb.

50

>   La **grande** fille parlait **rapidement**.
>   fem. sing.   adverb

>   The **tall** boy talked **rapidly**.
>
>   *Tall* modifies the noun *boy;* it is an adjective. *Rapidly* modifies the verb *talked* (it describes how the boy talked); it is an adverb.

>   Le **grand** garçon parlait **rapidement**.
>   masc. sing.   adverb

60

Remember that in English *good* is an adjective since it modifies a noun and *well* is an adverb since it modifies a verb.

>   The student writes *good* English.
>
>   *Good* modifies the noun *English;* it is an adjective.

>   The student writes *well*.
>
>   *Well* modifies the verb *writes;* it is an adverb.

Likewise, in French **bon** is an adjective meaning *good;* **bien** is the adverb meaning *well*.

>   The **good** students speak French **well**.

70

>   adjective   adverb

>   Les **bons** étudiants parlent **bien** le français.
>   masc. pl.   adverb

— *REVIEW* —

Circle the adverbs in the sentences below.
- Draw an arrow from the adverb to the word it modifies.

1. The students arrived early.

2. Paul learned the lesson really quickly.

3. The students were too tired to study.

4. He has a reasonably secure income.

5. Mary is a good student who speaks French very well.

CHAPTER

33

WHAT IS A CONJUNCTION?

A **CONJUNCTION** is a word that links two
or more words or groups of words.

He had to choose between good *and* evil.
                                     |
                              conjunction

They left *because* they were bored.
           |
        conjunction

IN ENGLISH

There are two kinds of conjunctions: coordinating and
subordinating.

- a **COORDINATING CONJUNCTION** joins words, phrases (groups
  of words without a verb), and clauses (groups of words
  with a verb) that are equal; it *coordinates* elements of
  equal rank. The major coordinating conjunctions are
  and, but, or, nor, for, and *yet.*

  good *or* evil
   | |
  word word

  over the river *and* through the woods
  |_____| |_____|
     phrase   phrase

  They invited us *but* we couldn't go.
  |_____| |_____|
     clause   clause

  In the last example, each of the two clauses, "they
  invited us" and "we couldn't go," expresses a complete
  thought; each clause is, therefore, a complete sentence
  which could stand alone. When a clause expresses a
  complete sentence it is called a **MAIN CLAUSE**. In the
  above sentence, the coordinating conjunction *but* links
  two main clauses.

- a **SUBORDINATING CONJUNCTION** joins a main clause to a
  dependent clause; it *subordinates* one clause to another.
  A **DEPENDENT CLAUSE** does not express a complete
  thought; it is, therefore, not a complete sentence and
  cannot stand alone. There are various types of depen-

dent clauses. A clause introduced by a subordinating conjunction is called a **SUBORDINATE CLAUSE**. Typical subordinating conjunctions are *before, after, since, although, because, if, unless, so that, while, that,* and *when.*

```
        subordinate clause        main clause
      ┌──────────────────┐   ┌──────────────┐
      Although we were invited, we didn't go.
      │
      subordinating
      conjunction
```

```
      They left because they were bored.
                   │
                   subordinating
                   conjunction
```

```
      He said that he was tired.
              │
              subordinating
              conjunction
```

In the above examples, "although we were invited," "because they were bored," and "that he was tired," are all subordinate clauses. They are not complete sentences and each is introduced by a subordinating conjunction.

Notice that the subordinate clause may come either at the beginning of the sentence or after the main clause.

IN FRENCH ────────────────────────────

Conjunctions must be memorized as vocabulary items. Just as adverbs and prepositions, conjunctions are invariable (i.e., they never change their form).

— *REVIEW* —

Circle the coordinating and subordinating conjunctions in the sentences below.
- Underline the words each conjunction serves to coordinate or to subordinate.

1. Mary and Paul were going to study French or Spanish.

2. She did not study because she was too tired.

3. Not only had he forgotten his ticket, but he had forgotten his passport as well.

CHAPTER

34

WHAT IS A PREPOSITION?

A PREPOSITION is a word that shows the relationship of one word (usually a noun or pronoun) to another word (usually another noun or pronoun) in the sentence.

prepositional phrase

Paul has an appointment *after* school.

preposition   object of preposition

The noun or pronoun following the preposition is called the OBJECT OF THE PREPOSITION. The preposition plus its object is called a PREPOSITIONAL PHRASE.

IN ENGLISH

Prepositions normally indicate location, direction, or time.

- prepositions showing location or direction

  Paul was *in* the car.
  Mary put the books *on* the table.
  The students came directly *from* class.
  Mary went *to* school.

- prepositions showing time and date

  French people go on vacation *in* August.
  On Mondays, they go to the university.
  I'm meeting him *at* 4:30 today.
  We're studying *before* taking the exam.
  Most people work *from* nine to five.

Other frequently used prepositions are: *during, since, with, between, of, about.*

IN FRENCH

You will have to memorize prepositions as vocabulary, paying special attention to their meaning and use. Prepositions are invariable; that is, they never change form (they never become plural, nor do they have a gender).

CAREFUL — Prepositions are tricky. Every language uses prepositions differently. Do not assume that the same preposition is used in French as in English, or even that a preposition will be needed in French when one is needed in English and vice versa.

ENGLISH	FRENCH
CHANGE OF PREPOSITION	
to be angry *with*	être fâché **contre** *(against)*
to be *on* the plane	être **dans** *(in)* l'avion
PREPOSITION	**NO PREPOSITION**
to wait *for*	attendre
to look *at*	regarder
NO PREPOSITION	**PREPOSITION**
to telephone	téléphoner à
to answer	répondre à

A dictionary will usually give you the verb and the preposition which follows it, when one is required.

Do not translate an English verb + preposition with a word-for-word French equivalent (see p. 22).

— REVIEW —

Circle the prepositions in the following sentences.

1. I shall call you towards the end of the week.

2. His family had come from Paris the year before we had.

3. The teacher walked around the room as she talked.

4. These days many men and women are working at home.

5. The garden between the two houses was very small.

CHAPTER

35

WHAT ARE OBJECTS?

OBJECTS are nouns or pronouns indicating towards what or whom the action of the verb is directed.

Paul writes a *letter*.
| |
verb   object

He speaks to *Mary*.
| |
verb   object

The boy left with *his father*.
| |
verb   object

We will study the three types of objects separately: direct object, indirect object, and object of a preposition. Since noun and pronoun objects are identified by using the same set of questions, we have limited the examples in this section to noun objects. For examples with pronoun objects see *What is an Object Pronoun?*, p. 111.

─────────────── **DIRECT OBJECT** ───────────────

IN ENGLISH

A direct object is a noun or pronoun which receives the action of the verb directly, without a preposition between the verb and the noun or pronoun object. It answers the question *whom?* or *what?* asked after the verb.[1]

Paul sees *Mary*.
Paul sees whom? Mary.
Mary is the direct object.

Paul writes *a letter*.
Paul writes what? A letter.
A letter is the direct object.

Verbs can be classified as to whether or not they take a direct object.

- a TRANSITIVE VERB is a verb which takes a direct object. It is indicated by the abbreviation *v.t.* (verb transitive) in dictionaries.

---

[1]In this section, we will consider active sentences only (see *What is Meant by Active and Passive Voice?*, p.160).

The boy *threw* the ball.

transitive   direct object

40

■ an **INTRANSITIVE VERB** is a verb that does not require a direct object. It is indicated by the abbreviation *v.i.* (verb intransitive) in the dictionary.

Paul *is sleeping.*

intransitive

IN FRENCH

As in English, a direct object is a noun or pronoun that receives the action of the verb directly, without a preposition. It answers the question **qui?** *(whom?)* or **quoi?** *(what?)* asked after the verb.

50

> *Paul sees* **Mary.**
> Paul voit **Marie.**
>> No preposition separates "Marie" from the verb "voit."
>> Therefore, *Marie* is a direct object.

> *Paul writes* **a letter.**
> Paul écrit **une lettre**.
>> No preposition separates "une lettre" from the verb "écrit."
>> Therefore, *une lettre* is a direct object.

60

As with English verbs, French verbs can be transitive or intransitive depending on whether or not they are followed by a direct object.

──────────── **INDIRECT OBJECT** ────────────

IN ENGLISH

An indirect object is a noun or pronoun which receives the action of the verb indirectly, with the preposition *to* relating it to the verb. It answers the question *to whom?* or *to what?* asked after the verb.

> She spoke *to her friends.*
>> She spoke to whom? Her friends.
>> *Her friends* is the indirect object.

70

> He gave the painting *to the museum.*
>> He gave a painting to what? The museum.
>> *The museum* is the indirect object.

IN FRENCH

As in English, an indirect object is a noun or pronoun which receives the action of the verb indirectly, with the preposition **à** *(to)* relating it to the verb. It answers the question **à qui?** *(to whom?)* or **à quoi** *(to what?)* asked after the verb.

80

Elle a parlé **à ses amis.**
*She spoke **to her friends.***

Il a donné le tableau **au musée.**
*He gave the painting **to the museum.***

Nouns that are indirect objects are easy to identify in French because they are always preceded by the preposition **à.**

SENTENCES WITH A DIRECT AND AN INDIRECT OBJECT

A sentence may contain both a direct object and an indirect object which can be either nouns or pronouns. In this section we shall speak only of nouns as objects because pronoun objects follow a different order.

IN ENGLISH

When a sentence has both a direct and an indirect object, the following two word orders are possible:

1. subject (S) + verb (V) + indirect object (IO) + direct object (DO)

> Paul gave his sister a gift.
> | | | | |
> S V IO DO

> *Who* gave a gift? Paul.
> *Paul* is the subject.

> Paul gave *what?* A gift.
> *A gift* is the direct object.

> Paul gave a gift *to whom?* His sister.
> *His sister* is the indirect object.

2. subject + verb + direct object + *to* + indirect object

> Paul gave a gift to his sister.
> | | | |
> S V DO IO

The first structure, under 1, is the most common. However, because there is no *"to"* preceding the indirect object, it is more difficult to identify its function than in the second structure.

Regardless of the word order, the function of the words in these two sentences is the same because they answer the same question. Be sure to ask the questions to establish the function of words in a sentence.

IN FRENCH

Unlike English, there is only one word order possible (structure 2) when a sentence has both a direct and an indirect object: subject + verb + direct object + à + indirect object.

Paul a donné **un cadeau à sa soeur**.

| | | | | | |
| S | V | DO | IO | | |

Paul gave his sister a gift.
Paul gave a gift to his sister.   130

────────────── **OBJECT OF A PREPOSITION** ──────────────

IN ENGLISH

An object of a preposition is a noun or pronoun which receives the action of the verb through a preposition other than *to*. (Objects of the preposition *to* are considered indirect objects and are discussed above.) It answers the question *whom?* or *what?* asked after the preposition.

Paul works *for Mary*.   140
   Paul works *for whom?* For Mary.
   Mary is the object of the preposition *for*.

The baby eats *with a spoon*.
   The baby eats *with what?* With a spoon.
   A spoon is the object of the preposition *with*.

IN FRENCH

As in English, an object of a preposition is a noun or pronoun that receives the action of the verb through a preposition other than **à** *(to)*. It answers the question **qui?** *(whom?)* or **quoi?** *(what?)* asked after the preposition.   150

Paul travaille **pour Marie**.
Paul works for Mary.

Le bébé mange **avec une cuillère**.
The baby eats with a spoon.

─────── **RELATIONSHIP OF A VERB TO ITS OBJECT** ───────

The relationship between a verb and its object is often different in English and French. For example, a verb may take a direct object in English and an indirect object in French, or an object of a preposition in English and a direct object in   160
French. Therefore, when you learn a French verb it is important to find out if it is followed by a preposition and if so which one. Your textbook, as well as dictionaries, will indicate when a French verb needs a preposition before an object (see p. 102).

Here are differences you are likely to encounter.

1. ENGLISH: object of a preposition → FRENCH: direct object

> *I am looking for the book.*
>> Function in English: object of a preposition
>> I am looking *for what*? The book.
>> *The book* is the object of the preposition *for*.
>
> Je cherche **le livre**.
>> Function in French: direct object
>> Je cherche **quoi**? Le livre.
>> The verb **chercher** is not followed by a preposition;
>> therefore, its object is a direct object.

Many common verbs require an indirect object or an object of a preposition in English, but a direct object in French.

*to listen **to***	écouter
*to look **at***	regarder
*to wait **for***	attendre

2. ENGLISH: direct object → FRENCH: indirect object

> *She phones **her friends** every day.*
>> Function in English: direct object
>> She phones *whom*? Her friends.
>> *Her friends* is the direct object.
>
> Elle téléphone **à ses amis** tous les jours.
>> Function in French: indirect object
>> Elle téléphone **à qui**? A ses amis.
>> The verb **téléphoner** is followed by the preposition **à**;
>> therefore, its object is an indirect object.

A few common verbs require a direct object in English and an indirect object in French.

to obey	obéir à
to resemble	ressembler à
to telephone	téléphoner à

3. ENGLISH: direct object → FRENCH: object of a preposition

> *Mary's parents remember **the war**.*
>> Function in English: direct object
>> Mary's parents remember *what*? The war.
>> *The war* is the direct object.
>
> Les parents de Marie se souviennent **de la guerre**.
>> Function in French: object of a preposition
>> Les parents de Marie se souviennent **de quoi**? De la guerre.
>> The verb **se souvenir** is followed by the preposition **de**;
>> therefore, its object is an object of the preposition **de**.

Here is another common verb which requires a direct object in English and an object of a preposition in French.

> *to enter*   entrer **dans**   210

Your ability to recognize the three types of objects is essential. With pronouns, for instance, a different French pronoun is used for the English pronoun *him* depending on whether *him* is a direct object (**le**) or an indirect object (**lui**). (See *What is an Object Pronoun?*, p. 111).

─────────────── **SUMMARY** ───────────────

The different types of objects in a sentence can be identified by establishing whether they answer a question which requires a preposition or not and, if so, which one.   220

DIRECT OBJECT — An object which receives the action of the verb directly, without a preposition.

INDIRECT OBJECT — An object which receives the action of the verb indirectly, through the preposition *to*.

OBJECT OF A PREPOSITION — An object which receives the action of the verb through a preposition other than *to*.

CAREFUL — Always identify the function of a word within the language in which you are working; do not mix English patterns into French.   230

— *REVIEW* —

Find the objects in the sentences below:
- Next to Q, write the question you need to ask to find the object.
- Next to A, write the answer to the question you just asked.
- Circle the kind of object it is: direct object (DO), indirect object (IO) or object of a preposition (OP).

1. The children took a shower.

   Q: _____

   A: _____   DO   IO   OP

2. They ate the meal with their friends.

   Q: _____

   A: _____   DO   IO   OP

   Q: _____

   A: _____   DO   IO   OP

3. He sent a present to his brother.

   Q: _____

   A: _____   DO   IO   OP

   Q: _____

   A: _____   DO   IO   OP

36

WHAT IS AN OBJECT PRONOUN?

An **OBJECT PRONOUN** is a pronoun used as an
object of a verb or a preposition.

> Paul saw *her*.
> Paul saw whom? Answer: Her.
> *Her* is the object of the verb *saw*.

Pronouns change according to their function in the sentence. Pronouns used as subjects are studied in *What is a
Subject Pronoun?*, p. 28. We use subject pronouns when we
conjugate verbs (see *What is a Verb Conjugation?*, p. 33).
Object pronouns are used when a pronoun is either a
direct object, indirect object, or object of a preposition
(see *What are Objects?*, p. 104).

IN ENGLISH

Most object pronouns are different from subject pronouns, but the same pronouns are used as direct objects,
indirect objects, or objects of a preposition.

	SUBJECT	**OBJECT**
SINGULAR		
1ST PERSON	I	me
2ND PERSON	you	you
3RD PERSON	he	him
	she	her
	it	it
PLURAL		
1ST PERSON	we	us
2ND PERSON	you	you
3RD PERSON	they	them

Let us look at a few examples.

> She saw *me*.
>   direct object → object pronoun

> He lent the car to *me*.
>   indirect object → object pronoun

> They went out with *me*.
>   object of a preposition → object pronoun

As you can see, the object pronoun is always placed after the verb.

IN FRENCH

As in English, the pronouns used as objects are different from the ones used as subjects. Unlike English, however, the form of an object pronoun often changes depending whether it is a direct, an indirect, or an object of a preposition.

In French, object pronouns are usually placed before the verb. Consult your textbook for the rules.

FRENCH DIRECT OBJECT PRONOUNS

First, you have to establish that the French verb takes a direct object. Remember that English and French verbs don't always take the same type of objects and that when working in French you have to establish the type of object required by the French verb (see p. 107).

Let us look at the French direct object pronouns to see how they are selected. Since the pattern of 1ˢᵗ and 2ⁿᵈ person direct object pronouns is different from the pattern of 3ʳᵈ person direct object pronouns, we have divided the French direct object pronouns into these two categories:

1ˢᵗ and 2ⁿᵈ persons singular and plural (me, you, and us)

The direct object pronouns of the 1ˢᵗ and 2ⁿᵈ persons are a question of learning vocabulary. Just select the form you need from the chart below.

	SUBJECT	DIRECT OBJECT	SUBJECT	DIRECT OBJECT
SINGULAR				
1ˢᵗ PERSON	je	me	*I*	*me*
2ⁿᵈ PERSON	tu	te	*you*	*you*
PLURAL				
1ˢᵗ PERSON	nous	nous	*we*	*us*
2ⁿᵈ PERSON	vous	vous	*you*	*you*

To simplify our examples we have used the verb **to see** (*voir*) because both the English and the French verbs take a direct object.

> *Paul sees **me**.*
> 1. Identify the verb: to see
> 2. What is the French equivalent: **voir**
> 3. Does the French verb need a preposition before an object: No

4. Function of pronoun in French: direct object
5. Selection: **me**

Paul **me** voit.

Paul sees **you.**
Paul **te** voit.
Paul **vous** voit.

Paul sees **us.**
Paul **nous** voit.

Establishing the function of **nous** and **vous** can be confusing. Not only are the same forms used as subject and object, but both subject and object pronouns are placed before the verb. In case of doubt, look at the verb. Remember that verbs agree with their subject. If **nous** is the subject, the verb will end in **-ons**; if it doesn't, **nous** is an object of some kind. The same is true with **vous.** If it is the subject of the verb, the ending of regular verbs will be **-ez.**

Vous **nous** voyez tous les jours.
> **Nous** cannot be the subject because the verb **voir** doesn't end in **-ons**. The subject of **voyez** can only be **vous.**
> Therefore, **nous** must be an object pronoun.

You see **us** *everyday.*

3rd person singular and plural (him, her, it and them) ———

The direct object pronouns of the 3rd person are a question of learning vocabulary, except for the pronoun *it* which changes depending on the gender of its ANTECEDENT; that is, the noun which it is replacing.

	SUBJECT	DIRECT OBJECT	SUBJECT	DIRECT OBJECT
SINGULAR MASCULINE	il	**le**	*he, it*	***him, it***
FEMININE	elle	**la**	*she, it*	***her, it***
PLURAL MASCULINE	ils			
FEMININE	elles	**les**	*they*	***them***

For our examples we have again used the verb **to see** *(voir)* because both the English and the French verbs take a direct object.

Do you see Paul? Yes, I see ***him.***
Voyez-vous Paul? Oui, je **le** vois.

*Do you see Mary? Yes, I see **her**.*
Voyez-vous Marie? Oui, je **la** vois.

*Do you see the girls? Yes, I see **them**.*
Voyez-vous les jeunes filles? Oui, je **les** vois.

It as a direct object requires that you establish the gender of the noun *it* refers to (i.e., its antecedent).

*Do you see the book? Yes, I see **it**.*
Voyez-vous le livre? Oui, je **le** vois.

> 1. Antecedent: **Livre** *(book)* is masculine.
> 2. Gender of *it:* masculine → **le**

*Do you see the table? Yes, I see **it**.*
Voyez-vous la table? Oui, je **la** vois.

> 1. Antecedent: **Table** *(table)* is feminine.
> 2. Gender of *it:* feminine → **la**

FRENCH INDIRECT OBJECT PRONOUNS

First, you have to establish that the French verb takes an indirect object. Remember that English and French verbs don't always take the same type of objects and that when working in French you have to establish the type of object required by the French verb (see p. 107).

Unlike noun indirect objects which are always preceded by the preposition **à** in French (see p. 105), pronoun indirect objects are not.

Let us look at the French indirect object pronouns to see how they are selected. Since the pattern of 1st and 2nd person indirect object pronouns is different from the pattern of 3rd person indirect object pronouns, we have divided the French indirect object pronouns into these two categories.

1st and 2nd persons singular and plural (me, you, and us) ———
The indirect object pronouns of the 1st and 2nd persons are the same as the direct object pronouns. Select the form you need from the chart below.

	SUBJECT	INDIRECT OBJECT	SUBJECT	INDIRECT OBJECT
SINGULAR				
1ST PERSON	je	me	*I*	*to me*
2ND PERSON	tu	te	*you*	*to you*
PLURAL				
1ST PERSON	nous	nous	*we*	*to us*
2ND PERSON	vous	vous	*you*	*to you*

To simplify our examples, we have chosen the verb *to speak to* (**parler à**) which takes an indirect object both in English and in French.

> *Paul speaks to me.*
>> 1. Identify the verb: to speak
>> 2. What is the French equivalent: **parler**
>> 3. Is the French verb followed by à: Yes
>> 4. Function of the pronoun in French: indirect object

Paul **me** parle.
   |
indirect object pronoun

> *Paul speaks to you.*
> Paul **te** parle.
> Paul **vous** parle.

> *Paul speaks to us.*
> Paul **nous** parle.

3rd person singular and plural (him, her, it and them) ————

There are two types of 3rd person indirect object pronouns, those referring to people and animals, and those referring to things and ideas.

	DIRECT OBJECT	INDIRECT OBJECT		DIRECT OBJECT	INDIRECT OBJECT
		PEOPLE	THINGS		
SINGULAR					
MASCULINE	le	lui		*him, it*	*to him*
FEMININE	la			*her, it*	*to her*
			y		*to it*
PLURAL					
MASCULINE	les	leur	y	*them*	*to them*
FEMININE					

1. The indirect object pronouns of the 3rd person referring to people are a question of learning vocabulary. The only way you can tell if **lui** refers to a male or female is from what has been said before.

 For the examples which follow, we have again used the verb *to speak to* (**parler à**) because both the English and the French verbs take an indirect object.

> *Are you speaking to Paul? Yes, I am speaking to him.*
>> 1. Identify the verb: to speak
>> 2. What is the French equivalent: **parler**

3. Does the French verb require the preposition à before an object? Yes
4. Function of the pronoun in French: indirect object
5. Type of antecedent: person *(Paul)*
6. Selection: **lui**

Parlez-vous à Paul? Oui, je **lui** parle.

Are you speaking to Mary? Yes, I am speaking to her.
Parlez-vous à Marie? Oui, je **lui** parle.

Are you speaking to Paul and Mary? Yes, I am speaking to them.
1 - 4. See above.
5. Type of antecedent: person *(Paul and Mary)*
6. Selection: **leur**

Parlez-vous à Paul et à Marie? Oui, je **leur** parle.

2. There is only one form of the 3rd person indirect object pronouns referring to things or ideas → **y**.

Are you answering the letter? Yes, I am answering it.
1. Identify the verb: to answer
2. What is the French equivalent: **répondre**
3. Does the French verb require the preposition à before an object? Yes
4. Function of the pronoun in French: indirect object
5. Type of antecedent: thing *(the letter)*
6. Selection: **y**

Répondez-vous à la lettre? Oui, j'**y** réponds.

Do you obey the laws? Yes, I obey them.
1. Identify the verb: to obey
2. What is the French equivalent: **obéir**
3. Does the French verb require the preposition à before an object? Yes
4. Function of the pronoun in French: indirect object
5. Type of antecedent: thing *(the laws)*
6. Selection: **y**

Obéissez-vous **aux** lois? Oui, j'**y** obéis.

$$à + les$$

FRENCH PRONOUNS AS OBJECTS OF A PREPOSITION

First, you have to establish that in French there is a preposition after the verb, and if so which one. Remember that English and French don't always use the same prepositions and that when working in French you have to establish the preposition used in French.

Let us look at the French object of a preposition pronouns to see how they are selected. Because the pattern of object of a preposition pronouns of the 1ˢᵗ and 2ⁿᵈ persons is different from the pattern of the object of a preposition pronouns of the 3ʳᵈ person, we have divided French object of a preposition pronouns into these two categories.

1ˢᵗ and 2ⁿᵈ person singular and plural (me, you, and us) ———

The 1ˢᵗ and 2ⁿᵈ person object of a preposition pronouns are a question of learning vocabulary. Select the form you need from the chart below and place it after the appropriate preposition.

	SUBJECT	OBJECT OF PREPOSITION	SUBJECT	OBJECT OF PREPOSITION
SINGULAR				
1ˢᵗ PERSON	je	prép. + moi	*I*	*prep. + me*
2ⁿᵈ PERSON	tu	prép. + toi	*you*	*prep. + you*
PLURAL				
1ˢᵗ PERSON	nous	prép. + nous	*we*	*prep. + us*
2ⁿᵈ PERSON	vous	prép. + vous	*you*	*prep. + you*

Here are a few examples.

> *Is the book for Paul ?   No, it's **for me.***
> *No, it's **for you.***
> *No, it's **for us.***

1. Identify the verb: to be
2. What is the French equivalent: **être**
3. Is the French verb followed by a preposition? Yes.
4. What preposition? **pour** *(for)*
5. Function of pronoun in French: object of preposition
6. Selection: **moi, toi (vous), nous**

Est-ce que le livre est **pour** Paul? Non, il est **pour moi.**
Non, il est **pour toi (vous).**
Non, il est **pour nous.**

3ʳᵈ person singular and plural (him, her, it and them) ———

There are two types of object of preposition pronouns:

- those referring to people and animals following any preposition
- those referring to things and ideas following the preposition **de** *(of, etc.)*. A noun referring to a thing preceded by any other preposition is not replaced. For instance, in French you cannot say "The book is on *it*" referring to *the table*; you must say "The book is on *the table*."

	Subject	**Object of Preposition**		**Subject**	**Object of Preposition**
		People	**Things** after de		
Singular					
masculine	il	prep. + **lui**		he, it	prep. + *him*
feminine	elle	prep. + **elle**		she, it	prep. + *her*
			en		*(of)* *it*
Plural					
masculine	ils	prep. + **eux**		they	prep. + *them*
feminine	elles	prep. + **elles**		they	prep. + *them*
			en		*(of)* *them*

1. The 3rd person object of a preposition pronouns referring to people and animals are a question of learning
vocabulary.

> *Is the book for Paul ? Yes, it is **for him**.*
> > 1. Identify the verb: to be
> > 2. What is the French equivalent: **être**
> > 3. Is the French verb followed by a preposition? Yes
> > 4. What preposition? **pour** *(for)*
> > 5. Function of pronoun in French: object of preposition
> > 6. Gender of antecedent: masculine *(Paul)*
> > 7. Selection: **lui**
>
> Est-ce que le livre est **pour** Paul? Oui, il est **pour lui**.

> *Is the book for Mary? Yes, it is **for her**.*
> > 1 - 5. See above.
> > 6. Gender of antecedent: feminine *(Mary)*
> > 7. Selection: **elle**
>
> Est-ce que le livre est **pour** Marie? Oui, il est **pour elle**.

> *Is the book for the boys? Yes it is **for them**.*
> > 1 - 5. See above.
> > 6. Gender of antecedent: masculine *(boys)*
> > 7. Selection: **eux**
>
> Est-ce que le livre est **pour** les garçons? Oui, il est **pour eux**.

> *Is the book for the girls? Yes it is **for them**.*
> > 1 - 5. See above.
> > 6. Gender of antecedent: feminine *(girls)*
> > 7. Selection: **elles**
>
> Est-ce que le livre est **pour** les filles? Oui, il est **pour elles**.

2. The 3rd person pronouns referring to things or ideas,
object of the preposition **de**, are replaced by the pronoun **en**.

Here are some examples:

*I liked the book so I am going to talk **about it**.*
    1. Identify the verb: to talk (to talk *about* → parler **de**)
    2. What is the French equivalent: **parler**
    3. Is the French verb followed by **de**: Yes
    4. Function of pronoun in French: object of preposition **de**
    5. Type of antecedent: thing *(book)*
    6. Selection: **en**
J'ai aimé le livre alors je vais **en** parler.

*I liked these books so I am going to talk **about them**.*
    1 - 6. See above.
J'ai aimé ces livres alors je vais **en** parler.

———— DISJUNCTIVE (STRESS) PRONOUNS ————

English object pronouns and the French object of a preposition pronouns, without the preposition, are also used as **DISJUNCTIVE** or **STRESS PRONOUNS**.

IN ENGLISH

A disjunctive pronoun, and not a subject pronoun, is used primarily in short answers with no verb.

    Who speaks French? *Me.*
                Him.
                Her.

IN FRENCH

As in English, a disjunctive pronoun, **LE PRONOM PERSONNEL TONIQUE** in French, and not a subject pronoun, is used in short answers with no verb.

    Qui parle français? **Moi.**
                Lui.
                Toi.
    *Who speaks French? **Me.***
                Him.
                You.

French disjunctive pronouns are also used, with the subject pronoun, for emphasis or contrast.

    ***He** is studying French, **I'm** studying Spanish.*
     | |
    subject pronoun   subject pronoun
    Lui il étudie le français, **moi** j'étudie l'espagnol.
     └┘   └┘
    stress pronoun +   stress pronoun +
    subject pronoun   subject pronoun

Consult your textbook for other uses of the French disjunctive pronouns.

————————— **SUMMARY**—————————

Below is a flow chart of the steps you have to follow to find the French equivalent of each English object pronoun. It is important that the steps be done in sequence, because each step depends on the previous one.

DO → Direct object in the French sentence

IO → Indirect object in the French sentence

OP → Object of a preposition or disjunctive pronoun in the French sentence.

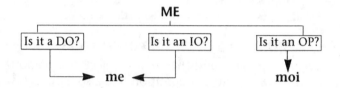

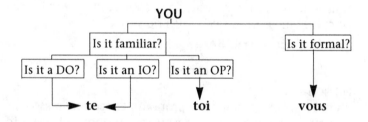

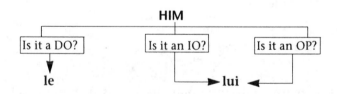

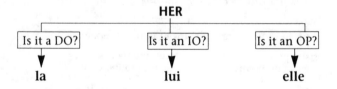

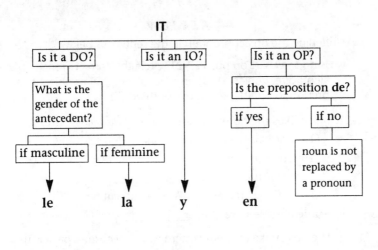

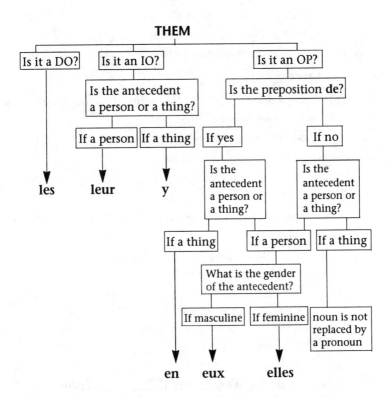

— *REVIEW* —

Underline the object pronoun in the sentences below.

- Using the chart on pp. 120-21, circle the correct French equivalent: direct object (DO), indirect object (IO) or object of a preposition (OP), person (P), or thing (T)

1. Mary likes the book and she reads it. *(to read → **lire**)*

   FUNCTION OF PRONOUN IN ENGLISH: DO IO OP

   FUNCTION OF PRONOUN IN FRENCH: DO IO OP

   ANTECEDENT IN ENGLISH: _____

   GENDER OF ANTECEDENT IN FRENCH: masculine

   Marie aime le livre et elle_____ lit.

2. The boy spoke to them yesterday. *(to speak to → **parler** à)*

   FUNCTION OF PRONOUN IN ENGLISH: DO IO OP

   FUNCTION OF PRONOUN IN FRENCH: DO IO OP

   TYPE OF ANTECEDENT: P T

   Le garçon_____a parlé hier.

3. Go with her. *(to go with → **aller avec**)*

   FUNCTION OF PRONOUN IN ENGLISH: DO IO OP

   FUNCTION OF PRONOUN IN FRENCH: DO IO OP

   Va avec_____

4. Did you answer his letters? No, we're answering them today. *(to answer → **répondre** à)*

   FUNCTION OF PRONOUN IN ENGLISH: DO IO OP

   FUNCTION OF PRONOUN IN FRENCH: DO IO OP

   ANTECEDENT IN ENGLISH: _____

   TYPE OF ANTECEDENT: P T

   Avez-vous répondu à ses lettres? Non, nous_____ répondons aujourd'hui.

5. Paul doesn't like exams. He is afraid of them. *(to be afraid of → **avoir peur de**)*

   FUNCTION OF PRONOUN IN ENGLISH: DO IO OP

   FUNCTION OF PRONOUN IN FRENCH: DO IO OP

   IS IT THE OBJECT OF PREPOSITION "DE": YES NO

   ANTECEDENT IN ENGLISH: _____

   TYPE OF ANTECEDENT: P T

   Paul n'aime pas les examens. Il_____a peur.

WHAT ARE REFLEXIVE PRONOUNS AND VERBS?

A **REFLEXIVE VERB** is a verb which is accompanied
by a pronoun, called a **REFLEXIVE PRONOUN**, which serves
"to reflect" the action of the verb back to the subject.

subject   reflexive pronoun = the same person

She *cut herself* with the knife.

reflexive verb

IN ENGLISH

Many regular verbs can take on a reflexive meaning by
adding a reflexive pronoun.

The child *dresses* the doll.

regular verb

The child *dresses herself.*

verb + reflexive pronoun

The reflexive pronouns end with *-self* in the singular and
-selves in the plural.

	SUBJECT PRONOUN	REFLEXIVE PRONOUN
SINGULAR		
1ST PERSON	I	myself
2ND PERSON	you	yourself
3RD PERSON	he	himself
	she	herself
	it	itself
PLURAL		
1ST PERSON	we	ourselves
2ND PERSON	you	yourselves
3RD PERSON	they	themselves

As the subject changes so does the reflexive pronoun,
because they both refer to the same person or object.

I cut *myself.*
Paul and Mary blamed *themselves* for the accident.

Although the subject pronoun *you* is the same for the
singular and plural, there is a difference in the reflexive

pronouns: *yourself* is used when you are speaking to one person (singular) and *yourselves* is used when you are speaking to more than one (plural).

> Paul, did you make *yourself* a sandwich?
> Children, make sure you wash *yourselves* properly.

Reflexive verbs can be in any tense: *I wash myself, I washed myself, I will wash myself,* etc.

IN FRENCH

As in English, French reflexive verbs **("LES VERBES PRONOMI-NAUX")** are formed with a verb and a reflexive pronoun.

Here are the French reflexive pronouns:

		REFLEXIVE PRONOUN
SINGULAR		
1ˢᵀ PERSON	me	*myself*
2ᴺᴰ PERSON	te	*yourself*
3ᴿᴰ PERSON	se	*himself, herself, itself*
PLURAL		
1ˢᵀ PERSON	nous	*ourselves*
2ᴺᴰ PERSON	vous	*yourself, yourselves*
3ᴿᴰ PERSON	se	*themselves*

In the dictionary, reflexive verbs are listed under the regular verb. For instance, under **laver** *(to wash)* you will also find **se laver** *(to wash oneself)*.

Look at the conjugation of **se laver**. Notice two things: 1. as in English, the reflexive pronoun changes according to the person of the conjugation, and 2. unlike English, the reflexive pronoun is placed before the verb.

	SUBJECT PRONOUN +	**REFLEXIVE PRONOUN +**	**VERB**
SINGULAR			
1ˢᵀ PERSON	je	me	lave
2ᴺᴰ PERSON	tu	te	laves
3ᴿᴰ PERSON	il / elle	se	lave
PLURAL			
1ˢᵀ PERSON	nous	nous	lavons
2ⁿᵈ PERSON	vous	vous	lavez
3ᴿᴰ PERSON	ils / elles	se	lavent

Reflexive verbs can be conjugated in all tenses. The subject and reflexive pronouns remain the same, regardless of the tense of the verb, only the verb form changes: **ils se** *laveront* (**futur**); **ils se** *sont lavés* (**passé composé**).

The compound tenses of reflexive verbs are always conjugated with the auxiliary **être** *(to be)*; however, the rules of agreement for the past participle of reflexive verbs are different from the rules of agreement of the past participle of regular verbs (see p. 57). Be sure to consult your French textbook for these rules.

Regular English verbs that can be made reflexive in English can also be made reflexive in French.

REGULAR VERB	REFLEXIVE VERB
Il **a coupé** le pain.	Il **s'est coupé** en se rasant.
He **cut** *the bread.*	*He* **cut himself** *shaving.*
Jean **a acheté** un livre.	Jean **s'est acheté** un livre.
John **bought** *a book.*	*John* **bought himself** *a book.*
Marie **a fait** le dîner.	Marie **s'est fait** une robe.
Mary **made** *dinner.*	*Mary* **made herself** *a dress.*

Reflexive verbs are common in French. There are many English expressions that are not reflexive in English, but whose French equivalent is a reflexive verb. You will have to memorize these idiomatic expressions.

to get up	se lever *(to get oneself up)*
to go to bed	se coucher *(to put oneself to bed)*
to wake up	se réveiller *(to wake oneself up)*
to be bored	s'ennuyer *(to bore oneself)*
to have fun	s'amuser *(to amuse oneself)*
to make a mistake	se tromper *(to mistake oneself)*
to stop	s'arrêter *(to stop oneself)*
to take a walk	se promener *(to walk oneself)*

In all the examples above, the French reflexive pronouns have a meaning equivalent to the English reflexive pronouns listed on p. 123 *(myself, yourself, himself,* etc.). This is not always the case. French reflexive pronouns can also indicate reciprocal action.

RECIPROCAL ACTION

IN ENGLISH

To express reciprocal action, that is, an action between two or more persons or things, English uses a regular verb followed by the expression "each other."

> The dog and the cat looked at *each other.*
> The expression "each other" tells us that the action of
> "looking" was reciprocal, i.e. the dog looked at the cat and
> the cat looked at the dog.

Our children call *each other* every day.
> The expression "each other" tells us that the action of "call-
> ing" is reciprocal, i.e. the various children call one another
> every day.

Since reciprocal verbs require more than one person or thing be involved, the verb is always plural.

IN FRENCH

French uses reflexive pronouns to express an action that is reciprocal.

> Le chien et le chat se regardaient.
> *The dog and the cat looked at **each other.***

> Nos enfants se téléphonent tous les jours.
> *Our children call **each other** every day.*

Context will often indicate to you if the meaning of the French pronoun is reflexive or reciprocal.

> Les danseurs se regardent dans le miroir.
> > The information "dans le miroir" leads us to believe that
> > they are looking at themselves. Therefore, se is reflexive.
> *The dancers look at **themselves** in the mirror.*
> |
>   reflexive

However, if no extra information is given, the meaning of the French sentence is ambiguous.

> Les danseurs se **regardent.**
> *The dancers **look** at themselves.* → **REFLEXIVE**
> *The dancers **look** at each other.* → **RECIPROCAL**

One way to avoid ambiguity, and to indicate that the meaning is reciprocal rather than reflexive, is to add an expression equivalent to "each other," such as **l'un l'autre"** (singular) or "**les uns les autres"** (plural).

> Le chien et le chat se regardent **l'un l'autre.**
> | | |
> sing.   sing.   sing.
> *The dog and the cat look at **each other.***

> Les danseurs se regardent **les uns les autres.**
> | | |
> plural   plural
> *The dancers look at **each other.***

Consult your textbook for detailed explanations.

— REVIEW —

I. Fill in the appropriate English reflexive pronoun in the English sentences.
   ▪ Fill in the equivalent French reflexive pronoun in the French sentences.

1. The children wash_____every evening.

   Les enfants _____ lavent tous les soirs.

2. Mary cuts _____ constantly.

   Marie _____ coupe constamment.

3. Mary, you cut _____ constantly.

   Marie, tu _____ coupes constamment.

4. We dress _____.

   Nous _____ habillons.

II. Fill in the appropriate English reflexive pronoun or the expression "each other."
   ▪ Circle "Rx" if the action is reflexive or "Rp" if the action is reciprocal.

1. The mother and son kissed _____.   Rx   Rp

2. Ambitious people push _____ to the limit.   Rx   Rp

3. Not to be punished, the children blamed
   _____ for breaking the mirror.   Rx   Rp

4. When something goes wrong
   I always blame _____.   Rx   Rp

5. Do you and your brother write _____.   Rx   Rp

WHAT IS A POSSESSIVE PRONOUN?

A **POSSESSIVE PRONOUN** is a word that replaces a noun
and indicates the possessor of that noun. The word
possessive comes from *possess,* to own.

> Whose house is that? It's *mine.*
>
> *Mine* replaces the noun *house,* the object possessed,
> and shows who possesses it, "me."

IN ENGLISH —————————————————————————

Here is a list of the possessive pronouns:

> **SINGULAR POSSESSOR**
>
> | | | |
> |---|---|---|
> | **1ST PERSON** | | mine |
> | **2ND PERSON** | | yours |
> | **3RD PERSON** { | MASCULINE | his |
> | | FEMININE | hers |
>
> **PLURAL POSSESSOR**
>
> | | |
> |---|---|
> | **1ST PERSON** | ours |
> | **2ND PERSON** | yours |
> | **3RD PERSON** | theirs |

Possessive pronouns only refer to the possessor, not to
the object possessed.

> My car is red; what color is John's? *His* is blue.
>
> 3rd pers. masc. sing.
>
> John's car is blue. What color is yours? *Mine* is white.
>
> 1st pers. sing.

> Although the object possessed is the same *(car),* different
> possessive pronouns *(his* and *mine)* are used because the
> possessors are different *(John* and *me).*

> Is that John's house? Yes, it is *his.*
> Are those John 's keys? Yes, they are *his.*

> Although the objects possessed are different *(house* and
> *keys),* the same possessive pronoun *(his)* is used because
> the possessor is the same *(John).*

IN FRENCH —————————————————————————

Like English, a French possessive pronoun refers to the
possessor. Unlike English, it also agrees, like all French pronouns, in gender and number with its **ANTECEDENT,** that is

with the person or object possessed. Also, the possessive
pronoun is preceded by a definite article which also agrees
in gender and number with the antecedent.

Let us look at some English sentences to see how to analyze them in order to find the correct form of the French
possessive pronoun.

> *Where are your books?* ***Mine*** *are in the living room.*
> 1. Find the possessor: *Mine* → 1st person singular.
> 2. Find antecedent: *Mine* refers to *books*.
> 3. Establish the gender and number of the French equivalent of
>   the antecedent: *(books)*.
> 4. Choose the ending of the possessive pronoun which corre-
>   sponds in gender and number to step 3 above.
> 5. Choose the definite article which corresponds in gender and
>   number to step 3 above.
>
> Où sont tes livres? **Les miens** sont dans le salon.
> 1. The first letter of the possessive pronoun **m-** indicates the 1ˢᵗ
>   person singular possessor *(mine)*.
> 2. The antecedent is **livres** *(books)*.
> 3. **Livres** is masculine plural.
> 4. The masculine plural ending is **-iens**.
> 5. The masculine plural definite article is **les**.

Let us look at the French possessive pronouns to see how
they are formed. The pattern of possessive pronouns for a
singular possessor is different from the pattern of possessive pronouns for a plural possessor. We have divided the
French possessive pronouns into these two groups.

─────────── Sɪɴɢᴜʟᴀʀ ᴘᴏssᴇssᴏʀ ───────────
mine, yours (tu-form), his, hers

In French, each of these possessive pronouns has four
forms depending on the gender and number of the
antecedent. To choose the proper form follow these steps.

1. Indicate the possessor. This will be shown by the first
   letter of the possessive pronoun. (They are the same
   initial letters as the possessive adjectives, see *What is a
   Possessive Adjective?*, p. 88.)

mine	**m-**
yours (**tu**-form)	**t-**
his ⎫	
hers ⎭	**s-**

2. Establish the gender and number of the antecedent and choose the definite article and the ending that corresponds to its gender and number.

- noun possessed is masculine singular → **le** + first letter of the possessor + **-ien**

A qui est ce **livre**?	C'est **le mien**.
masculine singular	C'est **le tien**.
	C'est **le sien**.
Whose book is that?	*It is mine.*
	It is yours.
	It is his (hers).

- noun possessed is feminine singular → **la** + first letter of the possessor + **-ienne**

A qui est cette **maison**?	C'est **la mienne**.
feminine singular	C'est **la tienne**.
	C'est **la sienne**.
Whose house is that?	*It is mine.*
	It is yours.
	It is his (hers).

- noun possessed is masculine plural → **les** + first letter of the possessor + **-iens**

A qui sont ces **livres**?	Ce sont **les miens**.
masculine plural	Ce sont **les tiens**.
	Ce sont **les siens**.
Whose books are those?	*They are mine.*
	They are yours.
	They are his (hers).

- noun possessed is feminine plural → **les** + first letter of the possessor + **-iennes**

A qui sont ces **lettres**?	Ce sont **les miennes**.
feminine plural	Ce sont **les tiennes**.
	Ce sont **les siennes**.
Whose letters are those?	*They are mine.*
	They are yours.
	They are his (hers).

3. Select the proper form according to the two steps above.

Let us apply these steps to some examples.

> *Mary is looking at her photos. John is looking at yours.*
> Marie regarde ses photos. Jean regarde **les tiennes**.
> 1. Possessor: 2ⁿᵈ person singular → **t-**
> 2. Noun possessed: **Photos** *(photos)* is feminine plural.
> 3. Selection: **les** + **t-** + **-iennes**

*Lend me your book. No, I'll lend you **hers.***
Prêtez-moi votre livre. Non, je vous prêterai **le sien.**
  1. Possessor: 3rd person singular → **s-**
  2. Noun possessed: **Livre** *(book)* is masculine singular.
  3. Selection: **le + s- + -ien**

────────────────── **PLURAL POSSESSOR** ──────────────────
ours, yours (vous-form), theirs

In French, each of these possessive pronouns has one form which is preceded by the definite article corresponding to the gender and number of the antecedent. To choose the proper form, follow these steps:

1. Indicate the possessor.

ours	**nôtre**
yours	**vôtre**
theirs	**leur**

2. Establish the gender and number of the antecedent and choose the definite article that corresponds to its gender and number.
   - noun possessed is masculine singular → **le**
   - noun possessed is feminine singular → **la**
   - noun possessed is plural → **les** + add an "s" to the possessor

3. Select the proper form according to the two steps above.

Let us apply these steps to some examples.

*I took my bag. Did you take **yours?***
J'ai pris mon sac. Avez-vous pris **le vôtre**?
  1. Possessor: 2nd person plural → **vôtre**
  2. Noun possessed: Sac (*bag)* is masculine singular.
  3. Selection: **le vôtre**

*I do not have my books, but Paul and Mary have **theirs.***
Je n'ai pas mes livres, mais Paul et Marie ont **les leurs**.
  1. Possessor: 3rd person plural → **leur**
  2. Noun possessed: **Livres** *(books)* is plural.
  3. Selection: **les + leur + - s**

Although **vôtre** is classified as "second person plural," it can refer to just one person when used as a formal form of address (see p. 29).

130

140

150

160

—————————— **SUMMARY** ——————————

Here is a chart you can use as a reference.

POSSESSOR SINGULAR		NOUN POSSESSED	
		SINGULAR	PLURAL
mine	MASC.	le mien	les miens
	FEM.	la mienne	les miennes
yours (**tu**-form)	MASC.	le tien	les tiens
	FEM.	la tienne	les tiennes
his, hers	MASC.	le sien	les siens
	FEM.	la sienne	les siennes

POSSESSOR PLURAL		NOUN POSSESSED	
		SINGULAR	PLURAL
ours	MASC.	le nôtre	les nôtres
	FEM.	la nôtre	
yours (**vous**- form)	MASC.	le vôtre	les vôtres
	FEM.	la vôtre	
theirs	MASC.	le leur	les leurs
	FEM.	la leur	

(margin numbers: 170, 180)

— *REVIEW* —

Underline the possessive pronouns in the sentences below.
- Draw an arrow from the possessive pronoun to its antecedent.
- Circle whether the antecedent is singular (S) or plural (P).
- Using the charts in this section, fill in the French possessive pronoun.

1. I won't take his car. I'll take mine.

   ANTECEDENT IN FRENCH: feminine   S   P

   Je ne prendrai pas sa voiture. Je prendrai _____

2. I'm not going with his parents. I'm going with hers.

   ANTECEDENT IN FRENCH: masculine   S   P

   Je ne vais pas avec ses parents. Je vais avec _____

3. Are you taking my book? No, I'm taking yours (familiar).

   ANTECEDENT IN FRENCH: masculine   S   P

   Prends-tu mon livre? Non, je prends _____

WHAT IS AN INTERROGATIVE PRONOUN?

An **INTERROGATIVE PRONOUN** is a word that replaces a noun
   and introduces a question. The word *interrogative*
   comes from *interrogate*, to question.

> *Who* is coming for dinner?
>
> replaces a person

> *What* did you eat for dinner?
>
> replaces a thing

   In both English and French, a different interrogative
pronoun is used depending on whether it refers to a "person" (human beings and live animals) or a "thing"
(objects and ideas). Also, the form of the interrogative pronoun often changes according to its function in the sentence: subject, direct object, indirect object, and object of
a preposition. We shall look at each function separately.

──────────────── **SUBJECT** ────────────────
(see *What is a Subject?*, p. 24)

IN ENGLISH

A different interrogative pronoun is used depending on
whether it refers to a person or a thing.

1. PERSON — ***Who*** is used for the subject of the sentence.

> *Who* speaks French?
>
> subject

2. THING — ***What*** is used for the subject of the sentence.

> *What* is on the table?
>
> subject

   An interrogative pronoun as subject is always followed
directly by the verb.

IN FRENCH

As in English, a different interrogative pronoun is used
depending on whether it refers to a person or a thing.

1. PERSON — **Qui** + verb *or* **Qui est-ce qui** + verb

> **Qui** parle français?
> **Qui est-ce qui** parle français?
> *Who speaks French?*

2. THING — **Qu'est-ce qui** + verb

> **Qu'est-ce qui** est sur la table?
> *What is on the table?*

As in English, an interrogative pronoun as subject is always followed directly by a verb.

───────────────── **DIRECT OBJECT** ─────────────────

(see p. 104 in *What are Objects?*)

IN ENGLISH

A different interrogative pronoun is used depending on whether it refers to a person or a thing.

1. PERSON — ***Whom*** is used for the object of the sentence.

> *Whom* do you know here?
> |
> direct object *(You* is the subject.)

Because *whom* is often replaced by *who* (ex: "*Who* do you know here?"), the form of the interrogative pronoun will not tell you if it is a subject or a direct object. It is only by analyzing the sentence that you will learn the function of the interrogative pronoun.

2. THING — ***What*** is used for the object of the sentence.

> *What* do you want?
> |
> direct object (*You* is the subject.)

IN FRENCH

As in English, a different interrogative pronoun is used depending on whether it refers to a person or a thing.

Notice that the forms with "**est-ce que**" take the normal word order, subject + verb, whereas the other forms are followed by an inversion, namely, verb + subject (see *What are Declarative and Interrogative Sentences?*, p. 45).

1. PERSON — **Qui est-ce que** + subject + verb *or* **Qui** + verb + subject

> **Qui est-ce que** vous connaissez?
> | |
>   subject + verb
> **Qui** connaissez-vous?
> | |
>   verb + subject
> ***Who(m)*** *do you know?*

40

50

60

70

2. THING — **Qu'est-ce que** + subject + verb *or* **Que** + verb + subject

> **Qu'est-ce que** vous voulez?
> |⎯⎯⎯⎯|
> subject + verb
>
> **Que** voulez-vous?
> |⎯⎯⎯|
> verb + subject
>
> *What do you want?*

⎯⎯ INDIRECT OBJECT AND OBJECT OF A PREPOSITION ⎯⎯
(see pp. 105-7 in *What are Objects?*)

IN ENGLISH

It is difficult to identify an English interrogative pronoun functioning as an indirect object or as an object of a preposition because it is often separated from the preposition of which it is the object. When a preposition is separated from its object and placed at the end of a sentence or question it is called a **DANGLING PREPOSITION**.

> *Who* did you speak *to?*
> |⎯⎯⎯⎯⎯⎯| |
> interr. pronoun preposition
>
> *Who* did you get the book *from?*
> | |
> interr. pronoun preposition

To enable you to establish if an interrogative pronoun is an indirect object or an object of a preposition, you will have to change the structure of the sentence so that the preposition is placed before the interrogative pronoun. This restructuring will not only make it easier for you to identify the function of the pronoun, but it will also establish the word order for the French sentence.

The following sentences have been restructured to avoid a dangling preposition.

> *Who* are you giving the book *to?*
> | |
> interr. pronoun preposition
> *To whom* are you giving the book?
> |
> indirect object
>
> *What* are you contributing *to?*
> | |
> interr. pronoun preposition
> *To what* are you contributing?
> |
> indirect object

Who are you going out *with?*
With whom are you going out?

object of the preposition *with*

What are you writing *with?*
With what are you writing?

object of the preposition *with*

The same form of the interrogative pronoun is used as an indirect object and as an object of a preposition. However, a different interrogative pronoun is used depending on whether it refers to a person or a thing.

1. PERSON — *Who (whom)* is used for indirect objects and objects of a preposition.

Who did you speak *to?*
To whom did you speak?

indirect object

Who did you get the book *from?*
From whom did you get the book?

object of preposition *from*

2. THING — *What* is used for indirect objects and objects of a preposition.

What did you pay *with?*
With what did you pay?

object of preposition *with*

IN FRENCH

As in English, there is no difference between the form of the interrogative pronoun as an indirect object (always preceded by the preposition à) and as an object of a preposition (always preceded by a preposition other than à). As in English, a different interrogative pronoun is used depending on whether it refers to a person or a thing.

1. PERSON — The preposition + **qui** + **est-ce que** + subject + verb *or* The preposition + **qui** + verb + subject

A qui est-ce que vous donnez le livre?

subject + verb

A qui donnez-vous le livre?

verb + subject

***To whom** are you giving the book?*

indirect object

Avec qui est-ce que vous sortez?
| |
subject + verb

Avec qui sortez-vous?
| |
verb + subject

With whom are you going out?
|
object of preposition *with*

2. THING — The preposition + **quoi** + **est-ce que** + subject + verb *or* The preposition + **quoi** + verb + subject

A quoi est-ce que vous contribuez?
| |
subject + verb

A quoi contribuez-vous?
| |
verb + subject

To what are you contributing?
|
indirect object

Avec quoi est-ce que vous écrivez?
| |
subject + verb

Avec quoi écrivez-vous?
| |
verb + subject

With what are you writing?
|
object of the preposition *with*

CAREFUL — Once again we remind you that some French verbs take direct objects, while the equivalent English verbs take an indirect object and vice-versa (see p. 107). Make sure that you determine the function of the pronoun in French.

─────────────── **SUMMARY** ───────────────

To choose the correct form of French interrogative pronouns, proceed with the following three steps:

1. Determine the function of the interrogative pronoun in the French sentence (subject, direct object, indirect object, or object of a preposition).
2. Establish whether the pronoun refers to a person or a thing.
3. Refer to the chart on the next page.

	Subject	**Direct Object**	**Indirect object and object of a preposition**
Person	*who* qui est-ce qui qui	*who(m)* qui est-ce que qui (+ inversion)	*preposition + who(m)* prép. + qui est-ce que prép. + qui (+ inversion)
Thing	*what* qu'est-ce qui	*what* qu'est-ce que que (+ inversion)	*preposition + what* prép. + quoi est-ce-que prép. + quoi (+ inversion)

———————— **"WHICH (ONE), WHICH (ONES)"** ————————

There is another interrogative pronoun which we will examine separately because it does not follow the same pattern as the ones above.

IN ENGLISH

Which (one), which (ones) are used in questions that request the selection of one *(which one,* singular) or more than one *(which ones,* plural) from a group that has already been mentioned. The words *one* and *ones* are often omitted. These interrogative pronouns can refer to both persons and things and they do not change according to their function; they may be used as a subject, direct object, indirect object, and object of a preposition.

All the teachers are here. *Which one* teaches French?
group mentioned   singular subject

I have two cars. *Which one* do you want to take?
group mentioned   singular direct object

The library has many books. *Which ones* do you want?
group mentioned   plural direct object

He has a group of friends. *Which ones* does he live with?
group mentioned   plural object of preposition *(with)*

IN FRENCH

As in English, these interrogative pronouns do not change according to function. Their form does change, however, according to gender and number. Their gender depends on the gender of their **ANTECEDENT** (i.e., the noun to which they refer), and their number depends on whether you want to say *which **one*** (singular) or *which **ones*** (plural).

	MASCULINE	FEMININE
SINGULAR	lequel	laquelle
PLURAL	lesquels	lesquelles

To choose the proper form, follow these steps:
1. Determine the antecedent.
2. Determine the gender of the antecedent.
3. Do you wish to say *which one* → singular or *which ones* → plural?
4. Select the correct French form from the above chart.

Let us apply these steps to some examples.

All the books are here. **Which one *is in French?***
Tous les livres sont ici. **Lequel** est en français?
  1. Antecedent: the books
  2. Gender: **Livres** *(books)* is masculine.
  3. Number: *One* is singular.
  4. Selection: masculine singular → **lequel**

I have two cars. **Which one *do you want to take?***
J'ai deux voitures. **Laquelle** veux-tu prendre?
  1. Antecedent: the cars
  2. Gender: **Voitures** *(cars)* is feminine.
  3. Number: *One* is singular.
  4. Selection: feminine singular → **laquelle**

I have many books. **Which ones *do you want to read?***
J'ai beaucoup de livres. **Lesquels** veux-tu lire?
  1. Antecedent: books
  2. Gender: **Livres** *(books)* is masculine.
  3. Number: *Ones* is plural.
  4. Selection: masculine plural → **lesquels**

Here are four girls; **which ones *do you want to speak* to?***
Here are four girls; **to which ones *do you want to speak?***
Voici quatre filles; **auxquelles** voulez-vous parler?
  1. Antecedent: girls
  2. Gender: **Filles** *(girls)* is feminine.
  3. Number: *Ones* is plural.
  4. Selection: feminine plural → à + **lesquelles** → **auxquelles**

There are two books. **Which one *are you speaking* about?***
There are two books. **About which one *are you speaking?***
Il y a deux livres. **Duquel** parlez-vous?
  1. Antecedent: books
  2. Gender: **Livres** *(books)* is masculine.
  3. Number: *One* is singular.
  4. Selection: masculine singular → de + **lequel** → **duquel**

250

260

270

280

— *REVIEW* —

Underline the interrogative pronouns in the questions below.
- Circle the interrogative pronoun's function in English and in French: subject (S) direct object (DO), indirect object (IO) or object of a preposition (OP). Restructure the English sentence, if necessary.
- Using the chart on p. 138, fill in the appropriate French equivalent.

1. Who came into the room?

   FUNCTION OF PRONOUN IN ENGLISH: S   DO   IO   OP

   FUNCTION OF PRONOUN IN FRENCH: S   DO   IO   OP

   _____ est entré dans la pièce?

2. Who did you speak to?

  RESTRUCTURE: _____

  to speak to → **parler à**

   FUNCTION OF PRONOUN IN ENGLISH: S   DO   IO   OP

   FUNCTION OF PRONOUN IN FRENCH: S   DO   IO   OP

   _____ est-ce que vous avez parlé?

3. What is she doing tonight?

  to do → **faire**

   FUNCTION OF PRONOUN IN ENGLISH: S   DO   IO   OP

   FUNCTION OF PRONOUN IN FRENCH: S   DO   IO   OP

   _____fait-elle ce soir?

4. Who are you calling?

  RESTRUCTURE: _____

  to call → **téléphoner à**

   FUNCTION OF PRONOUN IN ENGLISH: S   DO   IO   OP

   FUNCTION OF PRONOUN IN FRENCH: S   DO   IO   OP

   _____téléphonez-vous?

5. What did he cover the table with?

  RESTRUCTURE: _____

  to cover with→ **couvrir avec**

   FUNCTION OF PRONOUN IN ENGLISH: S   DO   IO   OP

   FUNCTION OF PRONOUN IN FRENCH: S   DO   IO   OP

   _____est-ce qu'il a couvert la table?

WHAT IS A RELATIVE PRONOUN?

A **RELATIVE PRONOUN** is a word used at the beginning of a
clause giving additional information about someone
or something previously mentioned.

clause
additional information about *the book*
I'm reading the book *which* the teacher recommended.

A relative pronoun serves two purposes:

1. As a pronoun it stands for a noun previously mentioned. The noun to which it refers is called the
ANTECEDENT.

   This is the boy *who* broke the window.

   antecedent of the relative pronoun *who*

2. It introduces a **SUBORDINATE CLAUSE**; that is, a group of
words having a subject and a verb which cannot stand
alone because it does not express a complete thought.
A subordinate clause is dependent on a **MAIN CLAUSE**;
that is, another group of words having a subject and a
verb which can stand alone as a complete sentence.

   main clause   subordinate clause
   Here comes the boy *who broke the window.*
   verb   subject subject verb

   A subordinate clause which starts with a relative pronoun is also called a **RELATIVE CLAUSE**. In the example
above, the relative clause starts with the relative pronoun *who* and gives us additional information about
the antecedent *boy.*

   Relative clauses are very common. We use them in
everyday speech without giving much thought as to
how we construct them. Relative pronouns allow us to
combine in a single sentence two thoughts which have
a common element.

   SENTENCE A   I met the teacher.
   SENTENCE B   He teaches French.
   COMBINED   I met the teacher *who* teaches French.

1

10

20

30

When sentences are combined with a relative pronoun, the relative pronoun can have different functions in the relative clause. It can be the subject, the direct object, the indirect object or the object of a preposition.

The selection of a relative pronoun often depends not only on its function in the relative clause, but also on whether its antecedent is a "person" (human beings and animals) or a "thing" (objects and ideas).

IN ENGLISH —————————————————————

In an English sentence, relative pronouns can sometimes be omitted.

> The book *that* I'm reading is interesting.
> |
>   relative pronoun

> The book I'm reading is interesting.
> |
>   relative pronoun omitted

IN FRENCH —————————————————————

The main difference between French and English relative pronouns is that relative pronouns must always be expressed in French sentences.

Since the selection of a relative pronoun depends on its function in the relative clause, we shall look at each function separately.

————————— **SUBJECT OF THE RELATIVE CLAUSE** —————————
(see *What is a Subject?*, p. 24)

IN ENGLISH

There are three relative pronouns that can be used as subject of a relative clause, depending on whether the relative pronoun refers to a person or a thing. When it is the subject of a relative clause, a relative pronoun is never omitted.

1. PERSON — *Who* or *that* is used as subject of the relative clause.

> She is the only student *who* answered all the time.
> She is the only student *that* answered all the time.
> | |
>   antecedent relative pronoun
>   subject of *answered*

2. THING — *Which* or *that* is used as subject of the relative clause.

> This is the book *which* is so interesting.
> This is the book *that* is so interesting.
> | |
> antecedent relative pronoun
>   subject of *is*

80

Notice that the relative pronoun subject is always followed by a verb.

IN FRENCH

There is only one relative pronoun that can be used as subject of a relative clause.

1. & 2. PERSON OR THING — **Qui** is used as the subject of a relative clause.

90

> *This is the student **who** answered.*
> Voici l'étudiant **qui** a répondu.
>
> *This is the book **which** is so interesting.*
> Voici le livre **qui** est si intéressant.

Notice that **qui** is always followed by a verb.

─────COMBINING SENTENCES: RELATIVE PRONOUN SUBJECT─────

IN ENGLISH

> SENTENCE A   The students passed the exam.
> SENTENCE B   They studied.

100

1. Identify the element the two sentences have in common.

> Both *the students* and *they* refer to the same persons.

2. The common element in the first sentence is called the ANTECEDENT of the relative pronoun; that is, the person or thing to which the relative pronoun refers. The relative pronoun always replaces the common element in the second sentence.

> *The students* is the antecedent.
> *They* will be replaced by a relative pronoun.

110

3. The relative pronoun in the relative clause has the same function as the word it replaces.

> *They* is the subject of *studied*. Therefore,
> the relative pronoun will be the subject of *studied*.

4. Choose the relative pronoun according to whether its antecedent is a person or a thing.

> *They* refers to *students*. Therefore, its antecedent
> is a person.

5. Select the relative pronoun.

Who or *that* is the subject relative pronoun referring to a person.

6. Place the relative pronoun at the beginning of the second sentence, thus forming a the relative clause.

who studied
that studied

7. Place the relative clause right after its antecedent.

The students *who studied* passed the exam.
The students *that studied* passed the exam.
        | └──┬──┘
    antecedent   relative clause

IN FRENCH

SENTENCE A   Les étudiants ont réussi à l'examen.
SENTENCE B   Ils ont étudié.

Follow the steps under in English above, skipping step 4.

Les étudiants **qui** ont étudié ont réussi à l'examen.
      | └──┬──┘
  antecedent   relative clause

──────── **DIRECT OBJECT OF THE RELATIVE CLAUSE** ────────
(see p. 104 in *What are Objects?*)

IN ENGLISH

There are three relative pronouns that can be used as direct object of a relative clause, depending on whether the relative pronoun refers to a person or a thing. When it is the direct object of a relative clause, a relative pronoun is often omitted.

1. PERSON — **Whom** or **that** is used as direct object of a relative clause.

This is the student *(whom)* I saw yesterday.
This is the student *(that)* I saw yesterday.
     | |
antecedent   direct object of *saw*

2. THING — **Which** or **that** is used as direct object of a relative clause.

This is the book *(which)* Paul bought.
This is the book *(that)* Paul bought.
     | |
antecedent direct object of *bought*

Notice that the relative pronoun as object is always followed by a noun or pronoun.

IN FRENCH　　　　160

There is only one relative pronoun that can be used as direct object of a relative clause. Unlike English the relative pronoun is never omitted.

1. & 2. PERSON OR THING — **Que (qu'** before a vowel) is used as direct object of a relative clause.

We have included the relative pronouns in the English sentences below to show you what the French relative pronoun relates to; however, since relative pronouns are often omitted in English, we have put them between parentheses.　　170

*This is the student (**whom**) he saw.*
Voici l'étudiant **qu'**il a vu.

*This is the book (**which**) I bought.*
Voici le livre **que** j'ai acheté.

Notice that **que** is always followed by a noun or pronoun.

— COMBINING SENTENCES: RELATIVE PRONOUN DIRECT OBJECT —

IN ENGLISH

　SENTENCE A　The French teacher is nice.　　180
　SENTENCE B　I met him here.

　1. Common element: *French teacher* and *him*
　2. Element to be replaced: *him*
　3. Function of *him*: direct object
　4. Antecedent: *the French teacher* is a person.
　5. Selection: *whom* or *that*
　6. Relative clause: *whom (that)* I met here
　7. Placement: antecedent *(the French teacher)* + relative clause

The French teacher *(whom)* I met here is nice.
The French teacher *(that)* I met here is nice.
　　|　　|_____|
　　antecedent　relative clause　　190

　When the relative pronoun *whom* or *that* is left out ("The French teacher I met today is nice"), it is difficult to identify the two clauses.

IN FRENCH

　SENTENCE A　Le professeur de français est gentil.
　SENTENCE B　Je l'ai rencontré ici.

Follow the steps under in English above, skipping step 4.

Le professeur de français **que** j'ai rencontré ici est gentil.　　200
　|　　　　　　　　　|_____|
　antecedent　　　　　relative clause

──INDIRECT OBJECT AND OBJECT OF A PREPOSITION── IN A RELATIVE CLAUSE

(see pp. 105-7 in *What are Objects?*)

A relative pronoun as indirect object is a relative pronoun object of the preposition *to* and a relative pronoun as object of a preposition is a relative pronoun object of a preposition other than *to*.

Mary is the person to *whom* he gave the present.

relative pronoun indirect object

Mary is the person with *whom* he went out.

relative pronoun object of a preposition

IN ENGLISH

It is difficult to identify the function of these relative pronouns in English because they are often separated from the preposition of which they are the object. When a preposition is separated from its object and placed at the end of a sentence it is called a **DANGLING PREPOSITION** (see p. 135).

Mary is the person *that* he went out *with*.

relative pronoun   dangling preposition

There are two relative pronouns used as indirect objects or as objects of a preposition in a relative clause, depending on whether the relative pronoun refers to a person or a thing. When it is the indirect object or the object of a preposition in a relative clause, a relative pronoun is often omitted.

1. PERSON — *Whom* is used as indirect object and as object of a preposition.

Here is the student to *whom* I was speaking.

antecedent   indirect object

Here is the student about *whom* I was speaking.

antecedent   object of preposition *about*

The above sentences are usually expressed as follows:

Here is the student I was speaking *to*.
Here is the student I was speaking *about*.

These sentences without a relative pronoun and with a dangling preposition have to be restructured in order to establish the function of the relative pronoun which will have to be expressed in the French sentences. To restructure the English sentences, follow these steps:

1. Identify the antecedent.
2. Place the preposition after the antecedent.
3. Add the relative pronoun *whom* after the preposition.

250

SPOKEN ENGLISH →	RESTRUCTURED
Here is the student	Here is the student
I was speaking *to*.	*to whom* I was speaking.
	indirect object of *was speaking*
Here is the student	Here is the student
I was speaking *about*.	*about whom* I was speaking.
	object of preposition *about*

2. THING — **Which** is used as indirect object and as object of a preposition.

260

Here is the museum he gave the painting to.

antecedent   dangling preposition

SPOKEN ENGLISH →	RESTRUCTURED
Here is the museum	Here is the museum
he gave the painting *to*.	*to which* he gave the painting.
	indirect object of *gave*

IN FRENCH

Relative pronouns used as indirect objects or as objects of a preposition are divided into two main groups discussed separately below: 1. relative pronouns objects of prepositions other than **de** *(of, etc.)*, and 2. relative pronouns objects of the preposition **de.**

270

Unlike English, no matter what its function, a relative pronoun is never omitted.

─────────── **FRENCH RELATIVE PRONOUNS** ───────────
OBJECTS OF PREPOSITIONS OTHER THAN "DE"

This group includes relative pronouns as indirect objects because they are objects of the preposition **à** *(to).*

280

1. PERSON — Preposition + **qui**

Here is the man **(that)** *I am talking to.*

antecedent

SPOKEN ENGLISH   →   RESTRUCTURED
Here is the man   Here is the man
I am talking *to*.   *to whom* I am talking.

Voici l'homme **à qui** je parle.

to talk to → **parler à**

2. THING — Preposition + **lequel**

Lequel must agree with the antecedent in gender and number. Also, following the preposition **à** *(to)* the initial **le-** and **les-** become **au-** and **aux-**.

*These are the pens **(that)** I write **with**.*

antecedent

SPOKEN ENGLISH   →   RESTRUCTURED
These are the pens   These are the pens
I write *with*.   *with which* I write.

Voici les stylos **avec lesquels** j'écris.

masc. pl.   masc. pl.

We refer you to your French textbook for other ways to express relative pronouns which are objects of prepositions other than **de**.

─────────── **FRENCH RELATIVE PRONOUNS** ───────────
OBJECTS OF THE PREPOSITION "DE"

There is one relative pronoun which is most commonly used when the verb is followed by the preposition **de**.

1. & 2. PERSON OR THING — **Dont** replaces the preposition **de** and the relative pronoun.

*Here is the man **(that)** I am speaking **about**.*

antecedent

SPOKEN ENGLISH   →   RESTRUCTURED
Here is the man   Here is the man
I am speaking *about*. *about whom* I am speaking.

Voici l'homme **dont** je parle.

to speak about → **parler de**

We refer you to your French textbook for other ways to express relative pronoun which are objects of the preposition **de**.

────── COMBINING SENTENCES: RELATIVE PRONOUN ──────
OBJECT OF A PREPOSITION

IN ENGLISH

SENTENCE A   Mary read the book.
SENTENCE B   I was speaking about it.

   1. Common element: *the book* and *it*
   2. Element to be replaced: *it*   330
   3. Function of *it:* object of the preposition *about*
   4. Antecedent: *The book* is a thing.
   5. Selection: *which*
   6. Relative clause: *about which* I was speaking
   7. Placement: antecedent *(book)* + relative clause

Mary read the book *about which* I was speaking.
           antecedent   relative clause

IN FRENCH

SENTENCE A   Marie a lu le livre.   340
SENTENCE B   J' en parlais.

Marie a lu le livre **dont** je parlais.

───────── **POSSESSIVE MODIFIER "WHOSE"** ─────────

IN ENGLISH

The possessive modifier *whose* is a relative pronoun which does not change its form regardless of its function or its antecedent.

This is the student *whose* mother came.
         antecedent   possessive modifying *mother*   350

Look at the house *whose* roof burned.
         antecedent   possessive modifying *house*

IN FRENCH

The French equivalent of the possessive modifier *whose* is **dont.**

This is the student **whose** *mother came.*
Voici l'étudiant **dont** la mère est venue.

Look at the house **whose** *roof burned.*   360
Regarde la maison **dont** le toît a brûlé.

──────── **SUMMARY** ────────
Here is a chart you can use as reference:

FUNCTION IN	ANTECEDENT	
RELATIVE CLAUSE:	PERSON	THING
SUBJECT	*who, that, which* qui	
DIRECT OBJECT	*whom, that, which* que	
OBJECT OF "DE"	*of (about, etc.) whom, which* dont	
OBJECT OF PREPOSITION (other than "de")	*preposition + whom* prép. + qui	*preposition + which* prép. + lequel, etc.
POSSESSIVE MODIFIER	*whose* dont	

370

To find the appropriate relative pronoun you must go through the following steps.

1. Find the relative clause.
   - restructure the English clause if there is a dangling preposition and
   - add the relative pronoun if it has been omitted
2. Establish the function of the relative pronoun in the French sentence:

   SUBJECT — If the relative pronoun is the subject of the English sentence, it will be the subject of the French sentence → **qui.**

   DIRECT OBJECT — If the French verb takes a direct object → **que** or **qu'.**

   OBJECT OF THE PREPOSITION "DE" — If the French verb is followed by the preposition **de** → **dont.**

   OBJECT OF A PREPOSITION OTHER THAN "DE" — If the French verb is followed by a preposition other than **de:**
   - if a person → preposition + **qui**
   - if a thing → preposition + appropriate form of **lequel**
3. Select the relative pronoun (see chart above).
4. Place the relative pronoun and its clause right after the antecedent.

Let us apply the steps outlined above to the following sentences:

*The plane **that** comes from Paris is late.*
   1. Relative clause: that comes from Paris
   2. Function of relative pronoun: subject of relative clause

380

390

400

3. Selection: **qui**
4. Antecedent: *plane* (**avion**)
5. Placement: antecedent *(avion)* + **qui** + clause

L'avion **qui** arrive de Paris est en retard.

Here are the books (that) I bought yesterday.
1. Relative clause: that I bought yesterday
2. Function of relative pronoun in French:
   direct object of **acheter** *(to buy)*
3. Selection: **que**
4. Antecedent: *books* (**livres**)
5. Placement: antecedent *(livres)* + **que** + clause

410

Voici les livres **que** j'ai achetés hier.

Notice the agreement of past participle **achetés** (masc. pl.) with the preceding direct object **que** referring to **livres** (masc. pl.), see pp. 57-8.

Where is the book (that) you need?
1. Relative clause: that you need
2. Function of relative pronoun in French:
   object of preposition **de** *(to need → avoir besoin de)*
3. Selection: **dont**
4. Antecedent: *book* (**livre**)
5. Placement: antecedent (**livre**) + **dont** + clause

420

Où est le livre **dont** vous avez besoin?

Where is the table (which) he's working on?

SPOKEN ENGLISH	→	RESTRUCTURED
Where is the table he's working *on?*		Where is the table *on which* he's working?

1. Relative clause: on which he is working
2. Function of relative pronoun in French: object of preposition **sur** *(on)* + thing *(table → une table → feminine singular)*
3. Selection: **sur laquelle**
4. Antecedent: *table* (**table**)
5. Placement: antecedent (**table**) + **sur laquelle** + clause

430

Où est la table **sur laquelle** il travaille?

That is the boy (that) she is playing with.

SPOKEN ENGLISH	→	RESTRUCTURED
That is the boy she is playing *with.*		That is the boy *with whom* she is playing.

440

1. Relative clause: with whom she is playing
2. Function of relative pronoun in French: object of the preposition **avec** *(to play with → jouer avec)* + person *(boy)*
3. Selection: **qui**

4. Antecedent: *boy* (**garçon**)
5. Placement: antecedent (**garçon**) + **avec qui** + clause
   Voici le garçon **avec qui** elle joue.

Relative pronouns are tricky to handle and this handbook provides only a simple outline. Refer to your French textbook for additional rules.

—— RELATIVE PRONOUNS WITHOUT ANTECEDENTS ——

There are relative pronouns that do not refer to a specific noun or pronoun. Instead, they refer to an antecedent which has not been expressed or to an entire idea.

IN ENGLISH

There are two relative pronouns that can be used without an antecedent: *what* and *which*.

What — does not refer to a specific noun or pronoun.[1]

I don't know *what* happened.
             |
         no antecedent
         subject

Here is *what* I read.
          |
      no antecedent
      direct object

Which — refers to an entire idea, not to a specific noun or pronoun.

She didn't do well, *which* is a pity.
                    |
     antecedent: the fact that she didn't do well
     subject of *is*

You speak many languages, *which* I envy.
                        |
     antecedent: the fact that you speak many languages
     direct object of *envy* (*I* is the subject)

IN FRENCH

When a relative pronoun does not have a specific antecedent, the pronoun **ce** *(that)* is added to act as the antecedent. It is followed by the relative pronoun appropriate to its function in the relative clause, creating a structure which is word-for-word "that which."

---

[1]The relative pronoun *what* (meaning *that which*) should not be confused with other uses of *what*; as an interrogative pronoun *(**What** do you want?* **Qu'est-ce que** vous voulez?, see p. 133), and as an interrogative adjective *(**What** book do you want?* **Quel** livre voulez-vous?, see p. 93).

Here are a few examples.

*Here is **what** happened.*
1. Relative clause: what happened
2. No antecedent: add **ce**
3. Function of relative pronoun in French: subject
4. Selection: **ce qui**

490

Voici **ce qui** est arrivé.

*Show me **what** you bought.*
1. Relative clause: what you bought
2. No antecedent: add **ce**
3. Function of relative pronoun in French: direct object
   of **acheter** *(to buy)*
4. Selection: **ce que**

500

Montrez-moi **ce que** vous avez acheté.

*I don't know **what** he is talking about.*
1. Relative clause: *what* he is talking *about* – Restructured:
   about what he is talking
2. No antecedent: add **ce**
3. Function of relative pronoun in French: object of
   preposition **de** *(to speak about* → **parler de)**
4. Selection: **ce dont**

Je ne sais pas **ce dont** il parle.

*He doesn't speak French, **which** will be a problem.*
1. Relative clause: which will be a problem
2. Antecedent: "he doesn't speak French" → add **ce**
3. Function of relative pronoun in French: subject
4. Selection: **ce qui**

510

Il ne parle pas français, **ce qui** sera un problème.

*To speak French well, that's **what** I want.*
1. Relative clause: what I want
2. Antecedent: "to speak French well" → add **ce**
3. Function of relative pronoun in French: direct object of
   vouloir *(to want)*
4. Selection: **ce que**

520

Bien parler français, voilà **ce que** je veux.

— *REVIEW* —

Underline the relative pronoun in the sentences below.
- Circle the antecedent.
- Circle the function of the relative pronoun: subject (S), direct object (DO), object of a preposition (OP), object of preposition **de** (OP**de**), or possessive modifier (PM).
- Using the chart on p. 150, fill in the French relative pronoun in the French sentences below.

1. I received the letter that you sent me.
   (to send → **envoyer**)

FUNCTION IN ENGLISH:	S	DO	OP	OP	PM
FUNCTION IN FRENCH:	S	DO	OP	OP**de**	PM

   J'ai reçu la lettre _____ vous m'avez envoyée.

2. That is the young woman who speaks French.
   (to speak → **parler**)

FUNCTION IN ENGLISH:	S	DO	OP	OP	PM
FUNCTION IN FRENCH:	S	DO	OP	OP**de**	PM

   Voici la jeune fille _____ parle français.

3. Here is the man with whom I travelled.
   (travel with → **voyager avec**)

FUNCTION IN ENGLISH:	S	DO	OP	OP	PM
FUNCTION IN FRENCH:	S	DO	OP	OP**de**	PM

   Voici l'homme avec _____ j'ai voyagé.

4. This is the book whose title I had forgotten.
   (to forget → **oublier**)

FUNCTION IN ENGLISH:	S	DO	OP	OP	PM
FUNCTION IN FRENCH:	S	DO	OP	OP**de**	PM

   Voici le livre _____ j'ai oublié le titre.

5. Paul is the student I spoke of.

   RESTRUCTURE: _____

   (to speak of → **parler de**)

FUNCTION IN ENGLISH:	S	DO	OP	OP	PM
FUNCTION IN FRENCH:	S	DO	OP	OP**de**	PM

   Paul est l'étudiant _____ j'ai parlé.

WHAT IS A DEMONSTRATIVE PRONOUN?

A DEMONSTRATIVE PRONOUN is a word that replaces a noun   [1]
as if pointing to it. The word *demonstrative*
comes from *demonstrate,* to show.

Choose a suit. *This one* is expensive. *That one* is not.
   antecedent   points to one suit   points to another suit

In English and French, demonstrative pronouns can be
used in a variety of ways.

───── **"THIS ONE, THAT ONE" AND "THESE, THOSE"** ─────   [10]

IN ENGLISH

The singular demonstrative pronouns are ***this (one)*** and
that (one); the plural forms are ***these*** and ***those.***

Here are my suitcases. *This one* is big ; *those* are small.
   antecedent   singular   plural

Choose a book. *Those* are in French, *that one* is in English.
   antecedent plural   singular

This (one), these refer to persons or objects near the speak-   [20]
er, and *that (one), those* refer to persons or objects further
away from the speaker.

IN FRENCH

Demonstrative pronouns agree in gender with their
ANTECEDENT; that is, the noun to which they refer. Their
number depends on whether they refer to one person or
object *(this one, that one)* or to more than one person or
object *(these, those).* Also, **-ci** is added to indicate persons
or objects close to the speaker and **-là** to indicate persons
or objects further away.   [30]

	MASCULINE	FEMININE
SINGULAR	celui	celle
PLURAL	ceux	celles

To choose the correct form, follow these steps:
   1. Determine the antecedent.
   2. Determine the gender the antecedent.

3. Number: *This one, that one* → singular; *these, those* → plural.
4. Based on steps 2 and 3 choose the correct form from the chart on p. 155.
5. Add **-ci** for *this* or *these* and **-là** for *that* and *those.*

Look at the following examples.

> *Which book did you read?* ***This one.***
> Quel livre as-tu lu? **Celui-ci.**
> 1. Antecedent: book
> 2. Gender: **Livre** *(book)* is masculine.
> 3. Number: This one → singular
> 4. Selection: **celui**
> 5. *This* —→ **-ci**

> *Which letter did you read?* ***That one.***
> Quelle lettre as-tu lue? **Celle-là.**
> 1. Antecedent: letter
> 2. Gender: **Lettre** *(letter)* is feminine.
> 3. Number: That one → singular
> 4. Selection: **celle**
> 5. *That* —→ **-là**

> *Which books did you read?* ***These.***
> Quels livres as-tu lus? **Ceux-ci.**
> 1. Antecedent: books
> 2. Gender: **Livres** *(books)* is masculine.
> 3. Number: These → plural
> 4. Selection: **ceux**
> 5. *These* —→ **-ci**

> *Which letters did you read?* ***Those.***
> Quelles lettres as-tu lues? **Celles-là.**
> 1. Antecedent: letters
> 2. Gender: **Lettres** *(letters)* is feminine.
> 3. Number: Those → plural
> 4. Selection: **celles**
> 5. *Those* —→ **-là**

──────── **TO SHOW POSSESSION: "CELUI DE"** ────────

IN ENGLISH

You can show possession with an apostrophe after the possessor, without repeating the person or object possessed mentioned in a previous sentence. The person or object possessed is the antecedent.

> Do you have a car? No, I use my *father's.*
> | |
>   antecedent   possessor + apostrophe

The word *car* is not repeated after *father;* it is understood.

IN FRENCH

Remember that the apostrophe structure to show possession does not exist in French (see p. 17). For the same reason that "my father's house" can only be expressed with the structure "the house *of* my father," the expression "my father's" can only be expressed with a structure that does not require an apostrophe. This structure word-for-word corresponds to "the one of" (singular antecedent) or "the ones of" (plural antecedent).

Do you have a car? No, I'm using my father's.   90

        | |
    antecedent   possessor + apostrophe
    singular   *"the one of* my father"

Do you have your keys? No, I'm using my father's.

        | |
    antecedent   possessor + apostrophe
    plural   *"the ones of* my father"

To show possession when the person or object possessed is not stated in the same sentence, French uses the demonstrative pronouns (without -**ci** or -**là**) + **de** *(of)*.

    100

To choose the correct form, follow these steps:

    1. Find the antecedent of *"the one"* or *"the ones."*
    2. Determine the gender and number of the antecedent.
    3. Based on step 2, select the form of the demonstrative pronoun (see chart p. 155).
    4. Add the preposition **de** *(of)*.

Let us apply these rules to the following examples:

*Which house are you selling? **My father's.***   110
    |
    antecedent   *"the one of my father"*
Quelle maison vendez-vous? **Celle de** mon père.
    1. Antecedent: house
    2. Gender & number: **Maison** *(house)* is feminine singular.
    3. & 4. Selection: **celle de**

*Which books are you taking? **The young man's.***
    |
    antecedent   *"the ones of the young man"*
Quels livres prenez-vous? **Ceux du** jeune homme.
    1. Antecedent: books
    2. Gender & number: **Livres** *(books)* is masculine plural.   120
    3. & 4. Selection: **ceux de**

————"THE ONE THAT": "CELUI QUI, CELUI QUE"————
(see *What is a Relative Pronoun?*, p. 141)

IN ENGLISH

The pronouns *the one* (singular antecedent) and *the ones* (plural antecedent), followed by the relative pronouns *that, which* or *who,* can start a relative clause giving us additional information about a person or object mentioned in a previous sentence. Since the relative pronouns *that, which* or *who* are often omitted in English, we have indicated them between parentheses.

> What book are you reading? *The one (that)* you gave me.
> > CLAUSE: *the one that you gave me* gives us
> > additional information about *the book.*
> > NUMBER: *The one* is singular.

> Which girls went to Paris? *The ones (who)* spoke French.
> > CLAUSE: *the ones who spoke French* gives us
> > additional information about *the girls.*
> > NUMBER: *The ones* is plural.

IN FRENCH

To express the English structure above, French uses the demonstrative pronouns followed by a relative pronoun. The demonstrative pronouns agree in gender and number with the antecedent. The relative pronoun is selected according to its function in the relative clause (see p. 142). Unlike English the relative pronoun must be stated.

To choose the correct form, follow these steps:

   A. Demonstrative pronoun *(the one, the ones)*
     1. Find the antecedent.
     2. Determine the gender and number of the antecedent.
     3. Select the French form according to the chart on p. 155.
   B. Relative pronoun *(that, which, who*—add to the English sentence if it has been omitted)
     1. Determine the function of the relative pronoun in the relative clause.
     2. Select the correct French form:
       ▪ the subject of the relative clause → **qui**
       ▪ the object of the relative clause → **que**

Let us apply these rules to the following examples:

> *What book are you reading? **The one (that)** you gave me.*
> Quel livre lis-tu? **Celui que** tu m'as donné.
> | └——┴——┘
> antecedent   dem. pronoun + relative pronoun
> masc. sing. masc. sing.   object

130
140
150
160

A. Demonstrative pronoun
  1. Antecedent: book
  2. Gender & number: **Livre** *(book)* is masculine singular.
  3. Selection: **celui**
B. Relative pronoun
  1. Function: *that* is the object of the relative clause.
    (Answers the question: "You gave *what?*" *You* is the subject.)   170
  2. Selection: **que**

Which girls went to Paris? ***The ones who spoke French.***
Quelles filles sont allées à Paris ? **Celles qui** parlaient français.

antécédent   dem. pronoun + relative pronoun
fem. pl.   fem. pl.   subject

A. Demonstrative pronoun
  1. Antecedent: girls
  2. Gender & number: **Filles** *(girls)* is feminine plural.
  3. Selection: **celles**
B. Relative pronoun   180
  1. Function: *who* is the subject of the relative clause.
  2. Selection: **qui**

— *REVIEW* —

Circle the demonstrative pronouns in the sentences below.
- Draw an arrow from the demonstrative pronoun to its antecedent.
- Circle if the antecedent is singular (S) or plural (P).
- Fill in the French demonstrative pronoun in the French sentences (see chart p. 155).

1. She did not buy that dress because she wants this one.

      ANTECEDENT IN FRENCH: feminine   S   P

Elle n'a pas acheté cette robe parce qu'elle veut _____.

2. My courses are more interesting than those.

      ANTECEDENT IN FRENCH: masculine   S   P

Mes cours sont plus intéressants que _____.

3. What book are you reading? The one I bought today.

      ANTECEDENT IN FRENCH: masculine   S   P

Quel livre lis-tu? _____ que j'ai acheté aujourd'hui.

CHAPTER

42

WHAT IS MEANT BY ACTIVE
AND PASSIVE VOICE?

1　**VOICE** in the grammatical sense refers to the relationship between the verb and its subject. There are two voices, the **ACTIVE VOICE** and the **PASSIVE VOICE.**

ACTIVE VOICE — A sentence is said to be in the active voice when the subject is the performer of the action of the verb. In this instance, the verb is called an **ACTIVE VERB.**

The teacher prepares the exam.
　　　　　|　　　　|　　　|
　　　　　S　　　　V　　　DO

10　Paul ate an apple.
　　|　|　　　|
　　S　V　　DO

Lightning has struck the tree.
　|　　└──┬──┘　　　|
　S　　　　V　　　　　DO

　　In all these examples the subject (S) performs the action of the verb (V) and the direct object (DO) is the receiver of the action (see *What is a Subject?*, p. 24 and *What are Objects?*, p. 104).

20　**PASSIVE VOICE** — A sentence is said to be in the passive voice when the subject is the receiver of the action of the verb. In this instance, the verb is called a **PASSIVE VERB.**

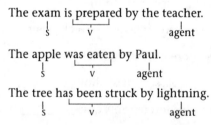

The exam is prepared by the teacher.
　|　　└──┬──┘　　　　　　|
　S　　　　V　　　　　　　agent

The apple was eaten by Paul.
　|　　└──┬──┘　　　|
　S　　　　V　　　agent

The tree has been struck by lightning.
30　|　　└──┬──┘　　　|
　S　　　　V　　　　agent

　　In all these examples, the subject is the receiver of the action of the verb. The performer of the action, if it is mentioned, is introduced by the word "by" and is called the **AGENT.**

IN ENGLISH ───────────────────────────

The passive voice is expressed by the verb *to be* conjugated in the appropriate tense + the past participle of the main verb. The tense of the passive sentence is indicated by the tense of the verb *to be*.

The exam *is prepared* by the teacher.   40
    |
  present

The exam *was prepared* by the teacher.
    |
  past

The exam *will be prepared* by the teacher.
  L─┬─┘
   future

IN FRENCH ───────────────────────────

As in English, a passive verb is expressed with the auxiliary **être** (*to be*) conjugated in the appropriate tense + the   50
past participle of the main verb. The tense of the passive sentence is indicated by the tense of the verb **être**.[1]

L'examen **est** préparé par le professeur.
     |
   present
*The exam **is** prepared by the teacher.*

L'examen **a été** préparé par le professeur.
   L─┬─┘
   past
*The exam **has been** (was) prepared by the teacher.*   60

L'examen **sera** préparé par le professeur.
     |
   future
*The exam **will be** prepared by the teacher.*

Because the auxiliary in the passive voice is always **être**, the past participles in a passive sentence always agree in gender and number with the subject (see p. 57).

Les vins français sont **appréciés** dans le monde entier.
    | |
subject → masc. pl.   past participle → masc. pl.
*French **wines** are **appreciated** the world over.*   70

---

[1]Verbs that take **être** as an auxiliary to form compound tenses in the active voice (see p. 57) do not have a passive voice since they are never followed by a direct object in the active voice. For example, **aller, partir, venir**, etc. cannot be made passive.

MAKING AN ACTIVE SENTENCE PASSIVE

The steps to change an active sentence to a passive sentence are the same in English and in French.

80

1. The direct object of the active sentence is made the subject of the passive sentence.

ACTIVE   The teacher prepares *the exam.*
↓   direct object
PASSIVE   *The exam* is prepared by the teacher.
                 subject

2. The tense of the verb of the active sentence is reflected in the tense of the verb *to be* in the passive sentence.

ACTIVE   The teacher *prepares* the exam.
↓   present
90
PASSIVE   The exam *is* prepared by the teacher.
                 present

ACTIVE   The teacher *prepared* the exam.
↓   past
PASSIVE   The exam *was* prepared by the teacher.
                 past

ACTIVE   The teacher *will* prepare the exam.
100
↓   future
PASSIVE   The exam *will be* prepared by the teacher.
                 future

3. The subject of the active sentence is made the agent of the passive sentence introduced with *by*. The agent is often omitted.

ACTIVE   *The teacher* prepares the exam.
↓   subject
PASSIVE   The exam is prepared *by the teacher.*
110
                                        agent

AVOIDING THE PASSIVE VOICE IN FRENCH

Although French has a passive voice, whenever possible French speakers try to avoid the passive construction by replacing it with an active one. This is particularly true for general statements; that is, when we don't know who is doing the action.

English *is spoken* in many countries.
We don't know who is speaking.

The New York Times *is sold* here.
We don't know who is selling.

There are two ways a passive sentence can be avoided in French:

1. using the **on** construction — The word **on** corresponds to the English indefinite pronoun *"one,"* as in the sentence, *"One* should eat when *one* is hungry."* To avoid a passive construction, French often makes *one* the subject of an active sentence, even in sentences where English speakers would never use such a construction.

English **is spoken** *in many countries.*
"one speaks"
On parle anglais dans beaucoup de pays.

The New York Times **is sold** *here.*
"one sells"
On vend le New York Times ici.

2. using the reflexive verb construction — The main verb of the sentence is changed from the English passive voice to the equivalent French reflexive verb (see *What are Reflexive Pronouns and Verbs?*, p. 123). This reflexive construction exists only in French and is meaningless in English.

English **is spoken** *in many countries.*
"speaks itself"
L'anglais se parle dans beaucoup de pays.

The New York Times **is sold** *here.*
"sells itself"
Le New York Times se vend ici.

CAREFUL — Make sure you distinguish between the auxiliary **être** + a past participle used to form a present tense in the passive voice and the auxiliary **être** + a past participle to form a past tense in the active voice.

For instance, **"est mangé"** *(is eaten)* is a present tense in the passive voice because the verb **manger** takes the auxiliary **avoir** to form the active past tenses (see p. 57), and "**est allé**" *(went)* is a past tense in the active voice because the verb **aller** takes the auxiliary **être** to form the active past tenses. Verbs that take the auxiliary **être** to form the active past tenses do not have a passive form.

— *REVIEW* —

Underline the subjects in the sentences below.
- Circle the performer of the action.
- Identify each sentence as active (Ac) or passive (Pa).
- Identify the tense of the verb: past (PP), present (P), future (F).

1. The cow jumped over the moon.   Ac Pa   PP   P   F

2. The bill was paid by Bob's parents.   Ac Pa   PP   P   F

3. The bank is transferring the money.   Ac Pa   PP   P   F

4. Everyone will be going away
during the vacation.   Ac Pa   PP   P   F

5. The spring break will be enjoyed
by all.   Ac Pa   PP   P   F

1. What is a Noun? 1. boy, classroom, teacher   2. textbook, painting, cover   3. Mary, Evans, Paris, class   4. lion, children   5. truth, fiction   6. kindness, understanding, world
2. What is Meant by Gender? 1. M   2. ?   3. F   4. ?   5. ?   6. F   7. ?
3. What is Meant by Number? The first letter corresponds to Column A, the second to Column B. 1. P P   2. P ?   3. S S   4. P P   5. P ?
4. What are Articles? 1. C, les   2. C, l'   3. C, des   4. C, une   5. N, de l'   6. N, le   7. C, un   8. N, de la   9. C, le
5. What is the Possessive? 1. the parents of some children   2. the color of the dress   3. the entrance of the school   4. the speed of a car   5. the covers of the books
6. What is a Verb? 1. purchase   2. were   3. enjoyed, preferred   4. ate, finished, went   5. was, see, struggle, get out   6. attended, celebrate
7. What is an Infinitive? 1. to do   2. study   3. to learn   4. leave   5. to travel
8. What is a Subject? 1. Q: "What rang?" the bell → sing. Q: "Who ran out?" the children → pl.   2. Q: "Who took the order?" one waiter → sing. Q: "Who brought the food?" another → sing.   3. Q: "Who voted?" the first-year students (or the students) → pl.   4. Q: "What is a beautiful language?" French → sing. Q: "What is difficult?" it → sing.
9. What is a Pronoun? The antecedent is in parentheses. 1. she (Mary), him (Peter)   2. they (coat, dress)   3. herself (Mary)   4. we (Paul, I)   5. it (book), it (table)
10. What is a Subject Pronoun? 1. je → 1st, sing.   2. vous → 2nd, pl.   3. nous → 1st, pl.   4. tu → 2nd, sing.   5. elles → 3rd, pl.   6. vous → 2nd, pl.   7. ils → 3rd, pl.
11. What is a Verb Conjugation? STEM: port-. CONJUGATION: je porte, tu portes, il (elle) porte, nous port**ons**, vous port**ez**, ils (or elles) port**ent**.
12. What are Auxiliary Verbs? 1. did   2. will   3. do   4. – (to have, **avoir**, is an auxiliary verb in French)
13. What are Affirmative and Negative Sentences? Words that indicate the negative are in italics. Words around which to place **ne...pas** are underlined. 1. We do *not* (don't) <u>want</u> to speak English in class.   2. He *does not* (doesn't) <u>do</u> his homework.   3. Helen <u>was</u> *not* (was*n't*) home this morning.   4. Paul <u>can</u>*not* (can*'t*) go to the restaurant with us.
14. What are Declarative and Interrogative Sentences? Words that indicate the interrogative are in *italics* I. 1. *Did* Paul and Mary study all evening?   2. *Does* his brother eat a lot?

3. *Do* the girl's parents speak French? II. 1. *Est-ce que* would precede: my mother and father went to the movies. 2. *n'est-ce pas* would follow: my mother and father went to the movies. 3. noun subject → mother and father; verb → went; pronoun that corresponds to the subject → they → *ils*

16. What is the Present Tense? 1. reads 2. is reading → *lit* 3. does read → *lit* 4. is reading → *lit*

17. What is a Participle? 1. am speaking 2. were studying 3. are bringing 4. will be trying

18. What is the Past Tense? IMPARFAIT: checked, handled, was crying, was, was leaving PASSÉ COMPOSÉ: went, arrived, ran, dropped, tried, ducked, grabbed, brought, comforted, went, left

19. What is the Pluperfect Tense? 1. (-1) → P; (-2) → PP 2. (-1) → P; (-2) → PP

20. What is the Future Tense? 1. ENGLISH: present, future FRENCH: future, future 2. ENGLISH: future, present FRENCH: future, future

21. What is the Future Perfect Tense? 1. (2), (1) 2. (1), (2). In French, the verbs marked (1) take the future perfect; the verbs marked (2) take the future.

23. What is the Imperative? I. 1. Study every evening. 2. Let's go to the movies once a week. II. 1. Don't sleep in class. 2. Let's not speak in class.

24. What is the Conditional? 1. C, I 2. PP, PC 3. I, I 4. F, P

27. What is a Descriptive Adjective? The noun or pronoun described is between parentheses. 1. young (man), French (newspaper) 2. pretty (she), new, red (dress) 3. interesting (it) 4. old (piano), good (music) 5. tired (Paul), long (walk)

28. What is Meant by Comparison of Adjectives? I. The noun modified is between parentheses.1. older (teacher) → C+ 2. less intelligent (he) → C- 3. as tall as (Mary) → C= 4. the worst (boy) → S 5. better (student) → C +

29. What is a Possessive Adjective? The noun described is between parentheses. 1. my (books), P → *mes* 2. your (car), sing. → *ta* 3. our (mother), sing. → *notre* 4. your (clothes), pl. → *vos*

30. What is an Interrogative Adjective? The noun modified is between parentheses. 1. which (courses), pl. → *quels* 2. what (city), sing. → *quelle*

31. What is a Demonstrative Adjective? I. The noun modified is between parentheses. 1. that (restaurant), sing. → *ce* 2. this (test), sing. → *cet* (examen starts with a vowel) 3. these (houses), pl. → *ces*

32. What is an Adverb? The word modified is between parentheses. 1. early (arrived)   2. quickly (learned), really (quickly), 3. too (tired)   4. reasonably (secure)   5. well (speaks), very (well)

33. What is a Conjunction? (The words to be circled are in *italics;* the words to be underlined are plain.) 1. Mary *and* Paul, French *or* Spanish.   2. She did not study *because* she was too tired.   3. Not only had he forgotten his ticket, *but* he had forgotten his passport as well.

34. What is a Preposition? 1. towards, of   2. from 3. around   4. at 5. between

35. What are Objects? 1. Q: "The children took what?" a shower → DO.   2. Q: "They ate what?" the meal → DO. Q: "They ate with whom?" their friends → OP.   3. Q: "He sent what?" a present → DO.   Q: "He sent a present to whom?" his brother → IO.

36. What is an Object Pronoun? 1. it, DO, DO, book → *le* 2. them, IO, IO, P → *leur*   3. her, OP, OP → *elle*   4. them, DO, IO, letters, T → *y*   5. them, OP, OP, yes, exams, T → *en*

37. What are Reflexive Prounouns and Verb? I. 1. themselves → *se*   2. herself → *se*   3. yourself → *te*   4. ourselves → *nous* II. 1. each other, Rp   2. themselves, Rx   3. each other, Rp 4. myself, Rx   5. each other, Rp

38. What is a Possessive Pronoun? 1. mine (car), sing. → *la mienne*   2. hers (parents), pl. → *les siens*   3. yours, (book), sing. → *le tien*

39. What is an Interrogative Pronoun? 1. who, S, S → *qui* or *qui est-ce qui*   2. who, to whom did you speak, IO, IO → *à qui* 3. what, DO, DO → *que*   4. who, whom are you calling, DO, IO → *à qui*   5. what, with what did he cover the table, OP, OP → *avec quoi*

40. What is a Relative Pronoun? The antecedent is between parentheses. 1. that (letter), DO, DO → *que*   2. who (woman), S, S → *qui*   3. whom (man), OP, OP → *qui*   4. whose (book), PM, PM → *dont*   5. Paul is the student of whom I spoke. Paul (student), OP, OPde → *dont*

41. What is a Demonstrative Pronoun? 1. this one (dress), sing. → *celle-ci*   2. those (courses), pl. → *ceux-là*   3. the one (book), sing. → *celui*

42. What is Meant by Active and Passive Voice? 1. cow, cow → Ac, PP   2. bill, parents → Pa, PP   3. bank, bank → Ac, P   4. everyone, everyone → Ac, F   5. spring break, all → Pa, F